Legends of Infamy: The Life Stories of Notorious Thieves

Shah Rukh

Published by Shah Rukh, 2024.

LEGENDS OF INFAMY: THE LIFE STORIES OF NOTORIOUS THIEVES

First edition. June 7, 2024.

Written by Shah Rukh.

Table of Contents

Prologue

In every shadowed corner of history, there lurks the tale of an audacious rogue, a cunning thief whose deeds transcended the mundane to etch their names into the annals of infamy. From the cobbled streets of Georgian London to the sun-scorched deserts of the American Southwest, from the rolling seas prowled by pirates to the darkened corridors of modern banks, the legends of these notorious figures captivate our imaginations and challenge our perceptions of law, morality, and heroism.

"Legends of Infamy: The Life Stories of Notorious Thieves" is a journey through the extraordinary lives of those who dared to defy the boundaries of society, who danced on the razor's edge between lawfulness and outlawry. These figures are more than mere criminals; they are the architects of some of history's most daring heists and schemes, their stories a mosaic of greed, ambition, and the relentless pursuit of freedom.

As we delve into the exploits of each character, we uncover not just the tales of their infamous crimes, but the complexities that drove them. What compels a person to step beyond the threshold of legality? Is it desperation, greed, the thrill of the chase, or a calculated decision to thumb their nose at a system they believe has failed them? Through their stories, we explore the human condition in its rawest form, stripped of pretense and laid bare in the pursuit of the ultimate score.

This book does not merely recount the deeds of these thieves; it seeks to understand them, to peel back the layers of myth and legend to reveal the human beings at their core. We will explore the motivations and machinations behind their crimes, the societies that produced them, and the often tragic, sometimes poetic, and occasionally triumphant fates that awaited them.

In "Legends of Infamy," you will meet the ruthless bandits who terrorized the Wild West, the suave con artists who swindled fortunes with a smile, and the daring pirates who ruled the high seas with an iron fist. You will discover the stories of those who have become folklore, their names synonymous with cunning and defiance. Their lives are not just tales of crime but narratives that challenge us to reflect on the nature of justice and the boundaries of morality.

So, step into the world where the line between right and wrong blurs, where heroes and villains wear the same cloak, and where the thrill of the heist beckons like a siren's song. These are the legends of infamy, the life stories of those who dared to dream beyond the confines of the ordinary and seized their place in history, not with a pen, but with the audacious stroke of their deeds.

Welcome to the world of notorious thieves. Welcome to the stories that refuse to be forgotten. Welcome to "Legends of Infamy."

Chapter 1: The Great Train Robbers

The Great Train Robbery, one of the most audacious and meticulously planned crimes of the 20th century, took place on the night of August 8, 1963. This legendary heist involved the theft of £2.6 million (equivalent to about £50 million today) from a Royal Mail train traveling from Glasgow to London. The robbery not only shocked the nation but also captivated the world, with its intricate planning, bold execution, and the subsequent drama of the investigation and trial. It stands as one of the most celebrated crimes in British history, often romanticized in popular culture.

The gang responsible for the Great Train Robbery consisted of 15 men, each chosen for their specific skills and roles. The mastermind behind the heist was Bruce Reynolds, a career criminal with a knack for organizing large-scale robberies. He was joined by Buster Edwards, Gordon Goody, and Charlie Wilson, among others, all of whom had extensive criminal backgrounds. The gang also included Roger Cordrey, a specialist in railway signaling, and Roy James, a getaway driver and former racing driver. Ronnie Biggs, who would later become the most famous of the robbers due to his dramatic escape and long time on the run, was a relatively minor player in the actual robbery.

The planning for the robbery took several months and was marked by meticulous attention to detail. The gang conducted extensive reconnaissance missions, studying the train's schedule, the layout of the railway line, and the security measures in place. They chose a remote section of the railway near Bridego Bridge in Buckinghamshire as the site for the heist. This location was selected because it was secluded and provided easy access for the getaway vehicles. The gang's preparations included renting Leatherslade Farm, a derelict property near the robbery site, to use as a hideout.

On the night of the robbery, the gang tampered with the railway signals at Bridego Bridge, causing the train to stop. They used a glove to cover the green light and placed a battery-operated red light over the signal, forcing the train to halt. As the train came to a stop, the robbers, wearing ski masks and gloves, swarmed the locomotive. They overpowered the driver, Jack Mills, and his assistant, David Whitby. Mills was struck on the head with an iron bar, sustaining severe injuries that would have long-term effects on his health.

The gang then detached the engine and the first two carriages, which contained the high-value packages, from the rest of the train. They moved the detached section about half a mile to Bridego Bridge, where they had parked their vehicles. At the bridge, the robbers unloaded 120 mailbags filled with cash, coins, and other valuables into waiting trucks. The entire operation was completed with military precision and took less than 30 minutes. The gang then made their way to Leatherslade Farm to divide the spoils.

Despite their careful planning, the robbers made several crucial mistakes that would lead to their eventual capture. They left behind fingerprints on the rail cars and at Leatherslade Farm. They had also underestimated the determination and resources of the police. The investigation, led by the Buckinghamshire Constabulary and assisted by Scotland Yard, was one of the largest manhunts in British history. The discovery of Leatherslade Farm was a significant breakthrough for the police. The farm was littered with evidence, including fingerprints, personal items, and even some of the stolen money. This evidence allowed the police to identify and track down the members of the gang.

The ensuing manhunt was relentless. Over the next few months, most of the gang members were arrested and brought to trial. The trial, held in 1964, was one of the longest and most publicized in British history. It lasted for 51 days and attracted massive media attention. The gang members were given harsh sentences, with most receiving 30 years in prison. The severity of the sentences reflected the British legal system's view of the robbery as a serious and unprecedented crime.

However, the story of the Great Train Robbery did not end with the convictions. Some members of the gang managed to escape from prison, adding another layer of drama to the saga. The most famous escapee was Ronnie Biggs, who scaled the wall of Wandsworth Prison in 1965 and fled to Brazil. Biggs lived a life of notoriety while on the run, becoming something of a folk hero. He remained a fugitive for 36 years before voluntarily returning to the UK in 2001, where he was promptly re-arrested and served out the remainder of his sentence.

The Great Train Robbery has had a lasting impact on popular culture. It has been the subject of numerous books, films, and documentaries. The audacity and scale of the robbery, combined with the dramatic manhunt and subsequent escapes, have ensured its place in criminal lore. The story also highlighted significant issues within the British transport and security systems of the time, leading to increased security measures for mail trains and better policing techniques.

Bruce Reynolds, often cited as the mastermind behind the robbery, later reflected on the heist as a product of its time—a daring and highly organized crime that was possible only in a pre-digital age. He and his gang took advantage of the limited technology and communication systems of the 1960s, executing a plan that would be almost impossible to replicate in today's world of advanced surveillance and forensic science.

The legacy of the Great Train Robbery extends far beyond the crime itself. It has come to symbolize both the ingenuity and the recklessness of the criminal mind, a fascinating chapter in the annals of criminal history that continues to captivate and intrigue. The story serves as a reminder of a bygone era when such a meticulously planned and executed robbery could capture the public's imagination and leave an indelible mark on history. The Great Train Robbery remains a testament to the audacity and ingenuity of those involved, as well as the tireless efforts of the police who eventually brought them to justice.

Chapter 2: Charles Ponzi

Charles Ponzi, one of the most infamous con men in history, was born Carlo Pietro Giovanni Guglielmo Tebaldo Ponzi on March 3, 1882, in Lugo, Italy. His name has become synonymous with financial fraud and deceit, largely due to the fraudulent investment scheme he orchestrated in the early 20th century, which came to be known as a "Ponzi scheme." Ponzi's life was a complex tapestry of ambition, deceit, and audacity, marked by his relentless pursuit of wealth through dubious means.

Ponzi came from a once-wealthy family that had fallen on hard times, which instilled in him a deep desire to restore his family's former glory and achieve financial success. In 1903, at the age of 21, he emigrated to the United States with dreams of making a fortune. He arrived in Boston with just $2.50, having gambled away the rest of his savings during the voyage. This inauspicious start was a harbinger of the tumultuous career that lay ahead.

Ponzi struggled to find steady employment in America. He took on a series of menial jobs, including dishwasher and waiter, but found it difficult to maintain employment due to his tendency to engage in petty theft and fraud. His early ventures into financial deceit began during these years, and he moved from city to city in search of opportunities.

In 1907, Ponzi moved to Montreal, Canada, where he worked for the Banco Zarossi, a bank that catered to Italian immigrants. The bank's founder, Luigi "Louis" Zarossi, was engaged in a form of financial fraud, using new deposits to pay interest to earlier depositors. This exposure to fraudulent banking practices left a lasting impression on Ponzi and laid the groundwork for his later schemes. When the bank collapsed, Ponzi was left destitute and resorted to forging a check, which led to his imprisonment for three years in a Canadian prison.

After his release, Ponzi returned to the United States and continued his pattern of petty crimes and scams, which included smuggling illegal Italian immigrants across the border. He was caught and served another term in a U.S. prison. Undeterred by his repeated incarcerations, Ponzi continued to dream of finding a legitimate way to achieve wealth.

In 1919, Ponzi stumbled upon an opportunity that he believed could make him rich beyond his wildest dreams. He discovered an arbitrage opportunity involving international postal reply coupons (IPRCs). These coupons were intended to allow someone in one country to pre-purchase postage for a reply from someone in another country. Ponzi realized that due to post-World War I economic imbalances, these coupons could be bought cheaply in Europe and redeemed for higher value in the United States. In theory, this arbitrage could yield a significant profit, and Ponzi saw it as the key to his financial success.

Ponzi began soliciting investments from friends and acquaintances, promising them a 50% return on their investment in just 45 days, or 100% in 90 days. He explained that his profits would come from the postal coupon arbitrage. At first, he used the money from new investors to pay returns to earlier investors, creating the illusion of a successful and profitable enterprise. This method of using new investors' funds to pay returns to earlier investors is the hallmark of what would later be called a Ponzi scheme.

As word of Ponzi's success spread, more and more people clamored to invest. By the summer of 1920, he was receiving as much as $250,000 a day, equivalent to over $3 million in today's money. Ponzi lived a lavish lifestyle, buying a mansion, luxury cars, and other expensive items, further fueling public fascination and trust in his scheme. The rapid influx of funds allowed him to expand his operation, and soon he had offices in several states.

However, despite the impressive façade, Ponzi's scheme was inherently unsustainable. The profits from postal reply coupons were nowhere near sufficient to cover the promised returns. The entire operation depended on an ever-increasing flow of new investments. As long as new money kept coming in, Ponzi could maintain the illusion of profitability. But any slowdown in new investments or an increase in withdrawals would expose the scheme's fraudulent nature.

In July 1920, the Boston Post began investigating Ponzi's operation. Skepticism about the legitimacy of his business grew, and a series of critical articles raised public doubts. The Massachusetts Securities Division also started scrutinizing his financial dealings. Despite Ponzi's efforts to reassure investors and maintain confidence, the scrutiny intensified, and withdrawals surged.

On August 10, 1920, Ponzi's scheme collapsed. State and federal authorities raided his offices, and it was revealed that he was insolvent. Investors had lost an estimated $20 million (equivalent to around $260 million today). Ponzi was arrested and charged with multiple counts of mail fraud. His trial was a media sensation, drawing widespread attention and outrage.

Ponzi pleaded guilty to mail fraud and was sentenced to five years in federal prison. After serving his federal sentence, he was tried and convicted on state charges, receiving an additional nine-year sentence. However, Ponzi's legal troubles were far from over. Upon his release from prison in 1934, he was deported to Italy as an undesirable alien.

Back in Italy, Ponzi struggled to regain his footing. He briefly worked for the government of Mussolini and later moved to Brazil, where he continued to engage in dubious financial schemes. However, he never achieved the same level of notoriety or financial success as he had in the United States. Charles Ponzi died in poverty in Rio de Janeiro on January 18, 1949, suffering from a stroke and subsequent cerebral hemorrhage.

Ponzi's legacy endures primarily through the term "Ponzi scheme," which is used to describe any fraudulent investment operation where returns to earlier investors are paid from the capital of newer investors rather than from profit earned by the operation. Ponzi schemes inevitably collapse when the flow of new investments dries up, leading to significant financial losses for the majority of investors.

The Great Depression of the 1930s, the Savings and Loan crisis of the 1980s, and the Bernie Madoff scandal of the 2000s are just a few examples of large-scale Ponzi schemes that have occurred since Charles Ponzi's time. These schemes highlight the enduring vulnerability of individuals to fraudulent investment schemes and the importance of regulatory oversight to protect investors.

Charles Ponzi's story is a cautionary tale of greed, deception, and the pursuit of wealth at any cost. His audacious fraud not only ruined the lives of countless investors but also left an indelible mark on the history of financial crime. Despite his ignominious end, Ponzi's name remains a powerful reminder of the perils of unchecked ambition and the enduring appeal of get-rich-quick schemes.

Chapter 3: Adam Worth

Adam Worth, often dubbed the "Napoleon of Crime," stands out as one of the most extraordinary and notorious criminals of the 19th century. His life story, full of daring heists, brilliant deceptions, and an elaborate web of criminal enterprises, continues to captivate historians and criminologists. Born in Germany in 1844, Worth's family immigrated to the United States during his early childhood, settling in Cambridge, Massachusetts. His formative years were marked by poverty, which likely influenced his later decisions. As a young man, he enlisted in the Union Army during the American Civil War. His military service was cut short, however, by a clerical error that listed him as killed in action after being wounded. Seizing the opportunity, Worth deserted the army and turned to a life of crime, thus beginning a career that would span continents and decades.

In the chaotic post-war era, Worth initially engaged in minor thefts and pickpocketing in New York City. However, his intelligence, charm, and organizational skills quickly distinguished him from other petty criminals. He meticulously planned his crimes, emphasizing precision and minimal risk, which set a standard for criminal operations. Worth's early forays into crime soon escalated to more sophisticated and lucrative endeavors. One of his first significant achievements was a bank robbery in New York, where his gang tunneled into the vault and made off with a considerable sum of money. This heist was notable not only for the amount stolen but also for the complexity and ingenuity of its execution.

As his reputation grew, so did the scale of his operations. Worth formed a gang of highly skilled criminals, orchestrating some of the most audacious heists of the time. Perhaps the most famous of these was the Manhattan Savings Institution robbery in 1878. Worth and his gang managed to steal approximately $500,000 in cash and securities, a staggering amount at the time. The heist was executed with such precision that it left law enforcement officials baffled and solidified Worth's status as a criminal mastermind. This event, among others, propelled him to the forefront of the criminal world and caught the attention of both the media and law enforcement.

Fearing the increased scrutiny and potential capture in the United States, Worth fled to Europe in the 1870s, establishing London as his new base of operations. In London, Worth continued his criminal activities, expanding them to include forgery, burglary, and even orchestrating the escape of fellow criminals from prison. His life in London was a complex duality; he lived as a respectable gentleman, married and fathered children, while simultaneously running a sophisticated criminal empire. His charm and wit allowed him to blend seamlessly into high society, which helped shield his illicit activities from suspicion.

One of Worth's most legendary crimes in Europe was the theft of Thomas Gainsborough's famous painting, "The Duchess of Devonshire," from Agnew's Art Gallery in 1876. This theft was one of the most sensational art heists of the time. The painting's disappearance created a media frenzy and stumped investigators for decades. Worth used the painting as leverage, a tool to negotiate and secure loans, showcasing his strategic acumen. The painting remained hidden for years, only coming to light after Worth's criminal empire began to crumble.

Worth's operations were not confined to England alone; his criminal network spanned across Europe and into America, involving a variety of illicit activities. He employed a network of operatives and informants, ensuring he was always one step ahead of the authorities. His ability to maintain a veneer of respectability was crucial to his success, allowing him to operate under the radar while law enforcement focused on less sophisticated criminals.

Despite his many successes, Worth's luck eventually ran out. In 1892, during a botched robbery in Liège, Belgium, he was finally captured. The arrest marked the beginning of the end for Worth. He was extradited to England, where he faced trial and was sentenced to seven years in prison. This incarceration effectively ended his criminal career, though his reputation as a master thief endured. Even behind bars, Worth's story continued to fascinate the public and law enforcement alike.

Worth was released from prison in 1897, having served his sentence. He spent his remaining years living quietly in London, far removed from the high-stakes world of crime he once dominated. He passed away in 1902, but his legacy lived on. Worth's life and exploits became the inspiration for various fictional characters, most notably Professor Moriarty, the arch-nemesis of Sherlock Holmes created by Arthur Conan Doyle. Worth's ability to outsmart the authorities, his preference for meticulous planning over brute force, and his remarkable adaptability set him apart as one of history's most intriguing and successful criminals.

The story of Adam Worth is a testament to the complexity of human behavior and the often fine line between brilliance and criminality. His life was a series of contradictions: a loving father and husband who led a double life as a criminal genius; a man of high society who orchestrated some of the most daring heists of his time. Worth's ability to manipulate and strategize with such finesse makes his story not just a tale of crime, but a study in human ingenuity and resilience. His enduring legacy as the "Napoleon of Crime" continues to be a subject of fascination and study, offering insights into the mind of a man who chose a life of crime and became one of its most notorious figures.

Chapter 4: Larry Phillips Jr. and Emil Mătăsăreanu

Larry Eugene Phillips Jr. and Emil Dechebal Mătăsăreanu are infamously remembered for their involvement in the 1997 North Hollywood shootout, a violent confrontation that left an indelible mark on American law enforcement and public consciousness. Their story is one of meticulous planning, heavy armament, and a brazen disregard for the law, culminating in one of the most intense gun battles in modern U.S. history.

Larry Phillips Jr. was born in 1970 in Los Angeles, California, to a family with a history of criminal activity. His father had multiple run-ins with the law, which seemingly influenced Phillips' own path. As a young man, Phillips was known for his physical fitness and fascination with bodybuilding, traits that would later play a role in his criminal endeavors. He had a penchant for meticulous planning and a belief in his own invincibility, qualities that would later manifest in his approach to armed robbery.

Emil Mătăsăreanu, born in 1966 in Romania, immigrated to the United States with his family in search of a better life. Mătăsăreanu's early years were marked by academic struggles and social isolation, which were compounded by the cultural and linguistic barriers he faced as an immigrant. Despite these challenges, he developed a passion for electronics and computers, skills that he later used in his criminal activities. Mătăsăreanu's intelligence and technical know-how complemented Phillips' physical prowess and strategic thinking, making them a formidable criminal duo.

The partnership between Phillips and Mătăsăreanu began in the early 1990s, with their initial criminal activities centered around burglaries and minor heists. However, their ambitions quickly grew, and they turned their attention to more lucrative targets: banks. Their modus operandi involved extensive planning and preparation. They were known to meticulously case their targets, studying security measures and response times. Their heists were characterized by military-style precision, heavily armed assaults, and an overwhelming show of force.

On February 28, 1997, Phillips and Mătăsăreanu executed their most infamous crime: the robbery of the Bank of America branch in North Hollywood. Armed with fully automatic rifles, an arsenal of high-capacity magazines, and clad in homemade body armor, they intended to subdue any resistance and escape with a substantial haul of cash. The robbery quickly spiraled out of control when a passing patrol officer spotted them entering the bank and called for backup.

As the duo exited the bank, they were met by a rapidly growing police presence. What ensued was a firefight of unprecedented scale. Phillips and Mătăsăreanu unleashed a barrage of gunfire, utilizing armor-piercing rounds that easily penetrated police vehicles and even the standard-issue body armor worn by officers. The intensity of the shootout was such that it necessitated the involvement of SWAT teams and a commandeering of high-powered firearms from a nearby gun store by desperate officers.

The firefight raged for nearly 45 minutes, during which Phillips and Mătăsăreanu demonstrated both their preparedness and their willingness to engage in a prolonged, deadly confrontation. Phillips, in particular, displayed a level of cool detachment, calmly reloading his weapon and returning fire with precision. Mătăsăreanu, while equally determined, was eventually incapacitated after sustaining multiple gunshot wounds. Phillips met a violent end, taking his own life after being critically injured by police fire. Mătăsăreanu, too, succumbed to his injuries, but not before an attempt to escape in a hijacked vehicle was thwarted by the police.

The aftermath of the North Hollywood shootout had far-reaching implications. The sheer firepower and body armor used by Phillips and Mătăsăreanu exposed significant gaps in police equipment and tactics. The incident led to widespread changes in law enforcement protocols, including the adoption of more powerful weaponry and improved body armor for police officers. It also sparked debates about gun control and the accessibility of high-capacity firearms and armor-piercing ammunition.

Beyond the immediate impact on law enforcement practices, the shootout became a cultural touchstone, referenced in media and popular culture as a symbol of extreme criminal audacity and the heroism of law enforcement officers under fire. The bravery of the officers, many of whom risked their lives despite being outgunned and under-protected, was widely celebrated. The event also underscored the potential for extreme violence in bank robberies, altering the way such crimes were perceived and handled.

Phillips and Mătăsăreanu's criminal legacy is a complex one. On the one hand, they are remembered as ruthless criminals who caused widespread fear and chaos. On the other hand, their actions inadvertently prompted significant advancements in police preparedness and response capabilities. Their story is a grim reminder of the potential for violence inherent in armed robbery and the lengths to which some criminals will go to evade capture.

The North Hollywood shootout remains one of the most extensively studied events in modern law enforcement history. It serves as a case study in tactical response, crisis management, and the evolution of police equipment and training. The incident has been the subject of numerous documentaries, books, and films, ensuring that the names Larry Phillips Jr. and Emil Mătăsăreanu will not soon be forgotten.

In examining the lives of Phillips and Mătăsăreanu, it is evident that their paths to infamy were shaped by a combination of personal circumstances, skills, and choices. Phillips' upbringing in a criminal environment and Mătăsăreanu's struggles as an immigrant both played roles in their eventual turn to a life of crime. Their partnership was a fusion of brute strength and technical expertise, a collaboration that proved deadly.

Ultimately, the story of Larry Phillips Jr. and Emil Mătăsăreanu is a chilling testament to the extremes of human behavior, the capacity for violence, and the enduring impact of one harrowing event on an entire nation. Their actions on that fateful day in February 1997 continue to resonate, serving as both a warning and a lesson in the ongoing battle between law enforcement and those who seek to operate outside the bounds of the law.

Chapter 5: Ronnie Biggs

Ronnie Biggs, an infamous figure in British criminal history, is best known for his involvement in the Great Train Robbery of 1963, a crime that captured the imagination of the public and remains one of the most talked-about heists in history. Ronald Arthur Biggs was born on August 8, 1929, in Stockwell, London, and his early life gave few clues to the notoriety he would later achieve. Raised in a working-class family, Biggs's formative years were marked by the economic hardships of the Great Depression and the upheaval of World War II. His early brushes with the law were relatively minor, but they set him on a path that would lead to one of the most audacious robberies ever committed.

By the early 1960s, Biggs had established himself within the London underworld, primarily through petty thefts and burglaries. His connections within this criminal milieu eventually led him to Bruce Reynolds, the mastermind behind the Great Train Robbery. Reynolds, along with a group of other seasoned criminals, had conceived a daring plan to intercept and rob the Royal Mail train traveling from Glasgow to London, which routinely carried large sums of money. The gang meticulously planned the heist for months, studying train schedules, practicing their tactics, and acquiring necessary tools and equipment, including a hijacked army surplus truck.

In the early hours of August 8, 1963, Biggs and his 14 accomplices executed their plan. The gang tampered with the track signals to stop the train in a remote area of Buckinghamshire. Once the train was halted, they overpowered the driver, Jack Mills, and used a stolen train engine to move the train to Bridego Bridge, where they had set up their operation. The robbers, all dressed in dark clothing and wearing masks, then proceeded to unload 120 sacks of cash, totaling £2.6 million, a staggering sum equivalent to about £53 million today.

The robbery itself was executed with military precision and minimal violence, although the train driver, Jack Mills, was struck on the head with an iron bar and left with lasting injuries. Despite the meticulous planning, the gang's post-robbery arrangements were less organized. They retreated to Leatherslade Farm, a pre-arranged hideout, where they had planned to lay low until the initial heat died down. However, they were forced to flee sooner than expected when the police closed in, leaving behind critical evidence that would eventually lead to their capture.

Biggs's share of the loot amounted to approximately £147,000, but his criminal life quickly began to unravel. He and several others were arrested within weeks of the robbery. In January 1964, Biggs was sentenced to 30 years in prison for his role in the heist. However, the story did not end there. In July 1965, after serving just 15 months, Biggs escaped from Wandsworth Prison in a meticulously planned breakout. With the help of friends on the outside, he scaled the prison wall using a rope ladder and jumped into a waiting van, disappearing into the London night.

Following his escape, Biggs went on the run, embarking on a global odyssey that would make him one of the most famous fugitives of the 20th century. Initially, he fled to Paris, where he underwent plastic surgery to alter his appearance and obtained false passports. From there, he traveled to Australia, where he lived for several years under various aliases, working as a carpenter and blending into the expatriate community. However, as the net began to close around him once more, he moved to Brazil in 1970, a country with no extradition treaty with the United Kingdom.

In Brazil, Biggs led a somewhat public life, even courting media attention. He capitalized on his notoriety, giving interviews and living openly in Rio de Janeiro. His life took another dramatic turn in 1974 when Scotland Yard detectives tracked him down. However, an unexpected twist in Biggs's favor came when his Brazilian girlfriend became pregnant. Under Brazilian law, he could not be extradited while he had a dependent child in the country, effectively securing his stay.

Biggs's time in Brazil was marked by a blend of semi-celebrity status and continued criminal activity. He remained a fugitive, yet he appeared in British tabloid newspapers and even recorded a song with the punk rock band the Sex Pistols in 1978, further cementing his legend. His ability to evade capture for so long was both a source of fascination and frustration for the British authorities.

Despite his relatively comfortable life in Brazil, Biggs never had access to the wealth he had once stolen. Over time, his health deteriorated, and by the late 1990s, he was in declining health, suffering from a series of strokes. In 2001, after 36 years on the run, Biggs voluntarily returned to the UK, driven by the need for medical care and a desire to spend his final years in his home country. Upon his return, he was immediately arrested and sent back to prison to complete his sentence. His health continued to decline, and after several years in custody, he was released on compassionate grounds in 2009, spending the remainder of his life in a care home until his death on December 18, 2013.

Ronnie Biggs's life story is a testament to both his audacity and his luck. His involvement in the Great Train Robbery and subsequent escape made him a folk hero to some, a symbol of the rebellious anti-establishment spirit of the 1960s. However, to others, he remained a criminal who caused significant harm and disruption. The robbery itself became a pivotal event in British criminal history, prompting changes in security measures and police procedures.

The cultural impact of the Great Train Robbery and Biggs's escapades cannot be overstated. The robbery has been the subject of numerous books, films, and television shows, each retelling the story with varying degrees of romanticism and realism. Biggs, with his larger-than-life persona and knack for staying in the public eye, became a central figure in these narratives.

Chapter 6: D.B. Cooper

D.B. Cooper is the pseudonym of an unidentified man who, on November 24, 1971, committed one of the most audacious and mysterious crimes in aviation history. His daring hijacking of a commercial airplane, subsequent ransom demand, and parachute escape have captivated the public and confounded authorities for decades. The case remains one of the greatest unsolved mysteries in FBI history, with numerous theories and extensive investigations failing to conclusively identify Cooper or determine his fate after the jump.

The saga began on the afternoon of November 24, 1971, when a man using the name Dan Cooper purchased a one-way ticket for Northwest Orient Airlines Flight 305 from Portland, Oregon, to Seattle, Washington. Described as a quiet, middle-aged man in his mid-forties, wearing a business suit, black tie, and carrying a briefcase, Cooper seemed unremarkable. Shortly after takeoff, however, he handed a note to flight attendant Florence Schaffner. Initially thinking it was a mere flirtation, Schaffner pocketed the note without reading it. Cooper then leaned toward her and whispered, "Miss, you'd better look at that note. I have a bomb."

Schaffner read the note, which stated Cooper had a bomb in his briefcase and demanded her to sit beside him. She complied, and Cooper discreetly opened his briefcase to reveal a jumble of wires and red sticks, reinforcing his threat. He dictated his demands to Schaffner: $200,000 in "negotiable American currency," four parachutes (two primary and two reserve), and a fuel truck standing by in Seattle to refuel the aircraft upon arrival. Schaffner conveyed the hijacker's instructions to the cockpit, and Captain William Scott informed air traffic control, who then alerted the authorities.

For the next several hours, Flight 305 circled the Seattle area as FBI agents scrambled to meet Cooper's demands. The ransom money was sourced from several Seattle-area banks, with each bill's serial number recorded for future tracking. The parachutes were obtained from a local skydiving school after initial confusion when military-issue parachutes were rejected by Cooper.

Once the plane landed at Seattle-Tacoma Airport, the hijacker allowed the passengers to disembark in exchange for the ransom and parachutes. However, he retained several crew members, including Captain Scott, to assist with the next phase of his escape plan. Cooper ordered the plane to be refueled and then provided detailed instructions for the subsequent flight: a course set for Mexico City, with the landing gear down, flaps set at 15 degrees, and the cabin depressurized. Additionally, he specified a flight altitude of 10,000 feet and a speed not exceeding 200 knots, conditions that would allow a safe parachute jump.

At approximately 7:40 p.m., Flight 305 took off again with Cooper and the skeleton crew aboard. As the plane flew southward, Cooper donned a pair of dark wraparound sunglasses, which would later become an iconic part of his image. Around 8:00 p.m., Cooper's final known actions unfolded. He instructed the remaining crew to stay in the cockpit and keep the door closed. Using the rear airstair of the Boeing 727, he made his exit somewhere over the dense, forested area of southwestern Washington, braving inclement weather and near-total darkness. This daring leap, with the money and parachutes, marked the beginning of one of the most extensive and enduring manhunts in American history.

The immediate aftermath saw a massive search effort initiated by the FBI, local law enforcement, and the military. Despite an exhaustive ground search and aerial reconnaissance, no trace of Cooper, his parachutes, or the money was found in the rugged terrain. The initial investigation produced few leads. Witnesses on the plane provided vague descriptions, and the hijacker's meticulous planning left little forensic evidence. The FBI, under the case name "NORJAK"

(Northwest Hijacking), launched one of its most comprehensive investigations, compiling a list of over 800 suspects by the late 1970s.

The investigation remained active for decades, with the FBI periodically releasing new information in hopes of jogging public memory or soliciting new leads. The most significant break in the case came in 1980 when a young boy named Brian Ingram found a decaying package containing $5,800 in cash, part of the ransom money, along the banks of the Columbia River near Vancouver, Washington. This discovery, although significant, raised more questions than answers. How did the money end up there? Was Cooper dead, or had he survived the jump only to lose part of his loot?

Over the years, numerous theories and suspects have emerged, each adding layers of intrigue to the case. Some of the most notable suspects included Richard Floyd McCoy, a former Green Beret and Vietnam veteran who executed a similar hijacking just months after Cooper's escape. McCoy, however, was later captured and killed in a shootout with the FBI, and there were significant differences between the two hijackings that cast doubt on his involvement in the NORJAK case.

Another prominent suspect was Duane Weber, a career criminal who, on his deathbed in 1995, allegedly confessed to his wife that he was D.B. Cooper. Although Weber's wife provided intriguing details, such as a recovered bank bag and a Northwest Airlines ticket, the FBI found no concrete evidence linking Weber to the crime. Similarly, Kenneth Christiansen, a former paratrooper and Northwest Airlines employee, was suggested as a possible suspect by his brother and a private investigator. However, the FBI dismissed him due to a lack of substantive evidence.

The FBI officially closed the case in July 2016, citing the need to focus on more pressing issues and the depletion of viable leads. Despite this, the legend of D.B. Cooper endures in popular culture, with books, documentaries, and fictionalized portrayals continuing to capture the public's imagination. The mystery of his true identity and fate remains a tantalizing puzzle, symbolizing the allure of the ultimate unsolved crime.

Cooper's escape has sparked countless debates among amateur sleuths and professional investigators alike. Some argue that he could not have survived the jump, pointing to the harsh conditions, the lack of specialized equipment, and the difficulty of navigating the terrain. Others believe he may have survived, citing the discovery of the money along the Columbia River as evidence that Cooper could have made his way to safety before succumbing to the elements or fading into obscurity.

Adding to the intrigue are the myriads of conspiracy theories that have surfaced over the years. Some speculate that Cooper had inside help, either from within the airline or among the passengers, allowing him to execute such a flawless plan. Others suggest government involvement or cover-ups, although no credible evidence supports these claims.

The D.B. Cooper case has also had lasting impacts on aviation security. In the aftermath of the hijacking, the Federal Aviation Administration mandated several changes to improve aircraft security. One of the most significant was the installation of "Cooper vanes," mechanical locks that prevent the aft staircases of Boeing 727s from being lowered mid-flight, effectively eliminating the method Cooper used to escape. Additionally, the case led to increased scrutiny and security measures in airports and on flights, setting the stage for the rigorous security protocols that are standard today.

Chapter 7: John Dillinger

John Dillinger, one of America's most infamous criminals, lived a life that encapsulated the tumultuous era of the Great Depression. Born on June 22, 1903, in Indianapolis, Indiana, Dillinger's early life did not suggest the notorious path he would eventually take. Raised in a middle-class family, his mother died when he was just three years old, and his father, a strict disciplinarian, struggled to manage him. Dillinger's rebellious nature and minor scrapes with the law during his youth were the initial signs of a troubled path.

In his teenage years, Dillinger's behavior grew increasingly delinquent. He dropped out of school and began associating with local troublemakers, which set the stage for his descent into more serious criminal activities. His first significant brush with the law came in 1924 when he attempted to rob a grocery store. The robbery was a failure, and Dillinger was quickly apprehended and sentenced to 10 to 20 years in the Indiana State Prison. It was here that Dillinger's transformation into a hardened criminal began. Prison exposed him to seasoned bank robbers and career criminals who taught him the skills and techniques he would later use to deadly effect.

Dillinger's prison term was marked by his strategic networking with other inmates. He formed alliances with men who would become his accomplices in future crimes, including Harry Pierpont and Homer Van Meter. These relationships were crucial in shaping his criminal career. While in prison, Dillinger meticulously planned future heists, learning from the seasoned criminals around him and honing his strategies. His time in prison solidified his resolve to pursue a life of crime upon release.

In May 1933, after serving nearly nine years, Dillinger was paroled, largely due to the lobbying efforts of his father and local sympathizers who believed he had been rehabilitated. However, any hopes of his reformation were quickly dashed. Upon his release, Dillinger immediately began organizing a series of bank robberies across Indiana and Ohio. His robberies were characterized by their boldness and precision, and Dillinger quickly gained notoriety as a masterful bank robber. His gang, known as the "Dillinger Gang," executed their heists with military-like precision, often outwitting local law enforcement and evading capture.

One of Dillinger's early heists involved robbing the New Carlisle National Bank in Ohio, where the gang made off with $10,000. Their methods were ruthless and efficient, involving the use of fast getaway cars, careful planning, and a readiness to use violence. Dillinger's ability to stay one step ahead of the law became a hallmark of his criminal career. His exploits captured the public's imagination, and he became something of a folk hero to those who saw him as a Robin Hood figure, striking back against the banks and institutions they blamed for their economic hardships.

However, Dillinger's criminal activities soon attracted the full attention of the FBI, which was then under the direction of J. Edgar Hoover. Hoover, keen to bolster the bureau's reputation and authority, made Dillinger's capture a top priority. The FBI's pursuit of Dillinger was relentless, involving extensive resources and coordination with local law enforcement agencies. Despite their efforts, Dillinger managed to evade capture multiple times, often through daring and cunning escapes that further cemented his legend.

One of the most dramatic episodes in Dillinger's life occurred in Crown Point, Indiana. In January 1934, after being captured and held in what was deemed an escape-proof jail, Dillinger managed to break out using a wooden gun he had meticulously carved and blackened with shoe polish. The escape was a stunning embarrassment for the authorities and a testament to Dillinger's audacity and resourcefulness. He stole the sheriff's car and drove across the state line, committing a federal offense that further escalated the manhunt against him.

Dillinger's escapades continued with a series of high-profile bank robberies and shootouts. His ability to elude capture became legendary, with newspapers eagerly chronicling his every move. The public was captivated by the cat-and-mouse game between Dillinger and the FBI, with many rooting for the outlaw. However, Dillinger's luck began to run out as the FBI closed in on him. In April 1934, he narrowly escaped a shootout with FBI agents in St. Paul, Minnesota, where his close associate, Baby Face Nelson, killed one agent and wounded several others.

The increasing pressure on Dillinger led him to seek refuge in Chicago, where he underwent plastic surgery to alter his appearance and avoid detection. Despite these efforts, Dillinger's days were numbered. In July 1934, the FBI received a tip from Anna Sage, a Romanian brothel owner who hoped to avoid deportation by aiding the authorities. She informed the FBI that Dillinger would be attending a screening of the film "Manhattan Melodrama" at the Biograph Theater on July 22, 1934.

FBI agents surrounded the theater and waited for Dillinger to emerge. As he exited, he was confronted by the agents. Dillinger attempted to flee but was shot multiple times, with a fatal bullet striking him in the back of the neck. He collapsed and died in the alley next to the theater. The dramatic end of John Dillinger marked the conclusion of one of the most intense manhunts in American history.

Dillinger's death did not end his legend. Instead, it solidified his status as an American folk hero and a symbol of rebellion against authority. The public's fascination with Dillinger continued to grow, fueled by numerous books, films, and documentaries that romanticized his life and exploits. His story became part of the cultural fabric of the United States, emblematic of the desperate and defiant spirit of the Great Depression era.

The Dillinger saga also had significant implications for law enforcement in the United States. The FBI's pursuit of Dillinger and other notorious criminals of the time, such as Bonnie and Clyde and Baby Face Nelson, led to significant changes in federal law enforcement practices. The bureau expanded its capabilities, adopted more modern investigative techniques, and enhanced its coordination with local law enforcement agencies. The pursuit of Dillinger helped to transform the FBI into a more effective and formidable force in combating organized crime and high-profile criminals.

Despite his criminal activities, Dillinger's legacy is complex. To many, he remains a symbol of defiance and resilience in the face of economic hardship and institutional corruption. His story is a reminder of the turbulent times during which he lived, a period marked by widespread poverty, social unrest, and a pervasive distrust of financial institutions. Dillinger's ability to capture the public's imagination speaks to the enduring allure of the outlaw figure in American culture, a figure who stands outside the law and challenges the established order.

In examining Dillinger's life, it is essential to acknowledge both the romanticized myth and the harsh realities of his criminal actions. While his exploits may have inspired admiration in some quarters, they also caused significant harm and suffering. The violence associated with his robberies, the lives lost, and the fear instilled in communities are undeniable aspects of his legacy. Dillinger's life and death underscore the complexities of the human condition, the thin line between heroism and criminality, and the powerful narratives that can emerge from times of great social upheaval.

John Dillinger's story remains a compelling chapter in American history, a tale of audacity, evasion, and ultimate downfall. His life, marked by a relentless pursuit of freedom and defiance against the system, continues to captivate and intrigue. Whether viewed as a villain, a hero, or something in between, Dillinger's legacy is a testament to the enduring fascination with those who challenge the boundaries of law and order in pursuit of their own path.

Chapter 8: Butch Cassidy and the Sundance Kid

Butch Cassidy and the Sundance Kid are two of the most iconic outlaws in American history, their names synonymous with the romanticized Wild West of the late 19th and early 20th centuries. Their legendary partnership and exploits have been immortalized in literature, film, and folklore, creating an enduring legacy that continues to captivate audiences today.

Butch Cassidy, born Robert LeRoy Parker on April 13, 1866, in Beaver, Utah, was the eldest of 13 children in a Mormon family. His parents, Maximillian Parker and Ann Campbell Gillies, were English immigrants who had converted to Mormonism. The family struggled with poverty, and young Robert, known affectionately as "Roy," began working at a young age. Despite his upbringing in a religious household, Parker soon found himself attracted to a life outside the confines of societal norms. His first brush with the law came as a teenager when he was accused of stealing a pair of overalls. Although he was acquitted, this incident marked the beginning of his criminal career.

Parker adopted the alias "Butch Cassidy" in honor of his mentor, Mike Cassidy, a cattle rustler who taught him the skills of the trade. By the 1880s, Butch had become involved in cattle rustling, horse stealing, and, eventually, bank and train robberies. He formed alliances with other outlaws and became the leader of the notorious Wild Bunch, a gang known for their meticulous planning and execution of heists. The Wild Bunch included a colorful array of characters, such as Elzy Lay, Harvey "Kid Curry" Logan, and Ben Kilpatrick. Their headquarters, the Hole-in-the-Wall in Wyoming, served as a remote hideout where they could evade law enforcement.

Sundance Kid, born Harry Alonzo Longabaugh in 1867 in Mont Clare, Pennsylvania, joined the Wild Bunch in the mid-1890s. Longabaugh, who earned his nickname after being jailed in Sundance, Wyoming, for horse theft, was known for his sharpshooting skills and cool demeanor. His partnership with Butch Cassidy became legendary, with the two men sharing a close bond and mutual respect. Together, they embarked on a series of audacious robberies that captured the public's imagination.

The Wild Bunch's most famous heist occurred on June 2, 1899, when they robbed a Union Pacific Overland Flyer train near Wilcox, Wyoming. The gang meticulously planned the operation, using dynamite to blow open the train's safe and making off with a substantial sum of money. This robbery, known as the Wilcox Train Robbery, became a defining moment in their criminal careers, cementing their reputation as the most successful outlaws of their time.

Despite their criminal activities, Butch Cassidy and the Sundance Kid were often portrayed as gentlemen bandits. They were known for their polite manners, reluctance to engage in unnecessary violence, and ability to charm those they encountered. This image was partly cultivated by the media, which romanticized their exploits and portrayed them as Robin Hood-like figures who stole from the rich and, if not exactly gave to the poor, at least lived by a code of honor that distinguished them from more ruthless criminals.

As law enforcement efforts intensified, Butch Cassidy and the Sundance Kid found themselves constantly on the run. The Pinkerton National Detective Agency, a private security firm, was hired to capture the outlaws. The Pinkertons, known for their relentless pursuit of criminals, employed a variety of tactics, including the use of wanted posters, informants, and advanced tracking methods. Despite these efforts, the Wild Bunch continued to evade capture, often fleeing to remote locations or hiding in their Hole-in-the-Wall hideout.

In 1901, facing increasing pressure from law enforcement, Butch and Sundance decided to leave the United States and seek refuge in South America. Accompanied by Etta Place, Sundance's girlfriend, they traveled to Argentina, where they purchased a ranch in Cholila, a remote area in the foothills of the Andes. For a few years, they lived a relatively quiet life, working as ranchers and attempting to leave their outlaw past behind.

However, the peace did not last. In 1905, after being implicated in a series of robberies, including the holdup of a Banco de Tarapacá y Argentino bank in Rio Gallegos, the trio fled to Bolivia. Their time in Bolivia was marked by a return to their old ways, with reports of their involvement in several robberies. The most famous of these was the robbery of a payroll transport near the mining town of San Vicente in November 1908.

The exact circumstances of their demise remain shrouded in mystery, but the most widely accepted account is that they were cornered by the Bolivian cavalry in San Vicente. After a brief shootout, it is believed that Sundance was mortally wounded, and Butch, not wanting to be captured, shot his friend before taking his own life. However, there are numerous theories and conflicting reports about their deaths, with some suggesting that one or both of them survived and continued their lives under new identities.

The legend of Butch Cassidy and the Sundance Kid grew exponentially after their deaths. In the early 20th century, their exploits became the subject of dime novels, which often exaggerated and romanticized their criminal careers. This trend continued into the mid-20th century, with Hollywood films further cementing their place in popular culture. The 1969 film "Butch Cassidy and the Sundance Kid," starring Paul Newman and Robert Redford, became a cultural phenomenon and introduced their story to a new generation. The film portrayed them as lovable rogues, emphasizing their camaraderie, wit, and daring escapades, while downplaying the more violent aspects of their criminal activities.

Historical research has continued to uncover new details about their lives, further enriching their story. Documents, photographs, and firsthand accounts have provided insights into their personalities, relationships, and motivations. Some researchers have even traveled to South America to trace their steps and uncover clues about their final days. Despite these efforts, many questions remain unanswered, contributing to the enduring fascination with their story.

The legacy of Butch Cassidy and the Sundance Kid is multifaceted. On one hand, they are remembered as outlaws who defied the law and lived life on their own terms. Their story is a testament to the spirit of rebellion and adventure that characterized the American West during the late 19th and early 20th centuries. On the other hand, their lives also reflect the harsh realities of a world where poverty, social upheaval, and rapid technological change drove many to desperation and crime.

The impact of their story extends beyond mere historical interest. Butch Cassidy and the Sundance Kid have become symbols of a bygone era, representing a time when the American frontier was still wild and untamed. Their legacy has influenced countless works of fiction, from Western novels to films and television series, shaping the popular image of the cowboy outlaw. They also serve as a reminder of the complex and often contradictory nature of historical figures, who can be both admired for their audacity and condemned for their lawlessness.

In recent years, the fascination with Butch Cassidy and the Sundance Kid has continued to grow, with new books, documentaries, and scholarly studies exploring different aspects of their lives. Their story has been analyzed through various lenses, including social history, criminology, and cultural studies, each offering new perspectives on why these two outlaws continue to captivate the public imagination.

Ultimately, the story of Butch Cassidy and the Sundance Kid is a rich tapestry of adventure, crime, friendship, and legend. It reflects the broader themes of American history, including the allure of the frontier, the challenges of law enforcement, and the enduring appeal of the outlaw hero. As their legend endures, Butch Cassidy and the Sundance Kid will continue to be celebrated and scrutinized, ensuring their place in the annals of American folklore for generations to come.

Chapter 9: Ma Barker

Ma Barker, born Arizona Donnie Clark on October 8, 1873, in Ash Grove, Missouri, is one of the most notorious figures in American criminal history, often depicted as the ruthless matriarch of the Barker-Karpis gang. Her life and legacy are surrounded by a mix of fact and legend, creating a complex and compelling narrative that has fascinated historians, writers, and the public for decades.

Arizona Clark, known as "Arrie," was born into a poor family and grew up in the rural Ozarks. Her early life was marked by hardship and limited opportunities, typical of many in her socioeconomic position during that era. She married George Barker, a tenant farmer, in 1892, and the couple had four sons: Herman, Lloyd, Arthur (nicknamed "Doc"), and Fred. The Barker family struggled to make ends meet, and their economic situation deteriorated further when George Barker, unable to cope with the challenges of supporting a large family, became increasingly absent and detached.

As a mother, Arrie was fiercely protective and indulgent of her sons, reportedly turning a blind eye to their early misdeeds. Her leniency and permissiveness are often cited as factors that contributed to their descent into a life of crime. The Barker boys began their criminal careers with petty thefts and escalated to more serious crimes, including burglary, robbery, and auto theft. Herman, the eldest, set a precedent for his younger brothers by engaging in increasingly violent and high-stakes criminal activities. He was involved in various armed robberies and eventually died in a police shootout in 1927, a fate that foreshadowed the violent ends that awaited his siblings.

By the late 1920s and early 1930s, the Barker brothers had become heavily involved in organized crime, forming the Barker-Karpis gang with Alvin Karpis, a notorious criminal with a reputation for meticulous planning and ruthlessness. The gang also included other notorious criminals such as Harry Campbell, Fred Goetz, and Volney

Davis. Ma Barker, as Arrie came to be known, was often portrayed as the mastermind behind the gang, a portrayal that has been debated by historians. Some argue that she was an active participant and leader, while others suggest she was more of a figurehead, with the real operational leadership provided by her sons and Karpis.

The Barker-Karpis gang became infamous for their involvement in a series of high-profile bank robberies, kidnappings, and murders. Their criminal activities spanned several states and often involved brutal violence. One of their most notorious crimes was the kidnapping of Edward Bremer, a wealthy banker from St. Paul, Minnesota, in January 1934. The gang demanded and received a ransom of $200,000 for Bremer's release, but the high-profile nature of the crime brought intense pressure from law enforcement. The gang's involvement in the Bremer kidnapping, along with the earlier abduction of William Hamm, another wealthy Minnesota businessman, marked the height of their criminal enterprise and contributed to their eventual downfall.

The FBI, under the leadership of J. Edgar Hoover, launched an extensive manhunt for the Barker-Karpis gang. Hoover, keen to bolster the bureau's reputation and authority, made their capture a top priority. The gang's ability to evade capture for several years despite the growing pressure from law enforcement was a testament to their cunning and resourcefulness. They utilized various hideouts, safe houses, and connections within the criminal underworld to stay one step ahead of the authorities.

Ma Barker's role in the gang has been a subject of much debate and myth-making. The FBI and popular media often depicted her as the cunning and ruthless leader of the gang, a portrayal that has been disputed by some historians. Critics argue that she was more of a matronly figure who provided moral support and a semblance of normalcy for her sons rather than an active participant in their criminal activities. According to Alvin Karpis, who survived to write his memoirs, Ma Barker did not have the criminal intelligence or organizational skills attributed to her by the FBI. Karpis described her as a loving mother who traveled with her sons to provide them with home-cooked meals and comfort but had little involvement in planning or executing their crimes.

Regardless of the true extent of her involvement, Ma Barker's association with the gang made her a target for law enforcement. The end of her life came on January 16, 1935, in a dramatic and violent showdown with the FBI at a rented house in Ocklawaha, Florida. Acting on a tip, FBI agents surrounded the house where Ma Barker and her son Fred were staying. After a prolonged gun battle, both Ma and Fred were killed. The FBI claimed that Ma Barker died with a machine gun in her hands, a detail that has been questioned by some historians who suggest it was part of Hoover's effort to craft a narrative that emphasized her as a dangerous criminal mastermind.

The deaths of Ma and Fred Barker marked the end of the Barker-Karpis gang as a significant criminal enterprise. Alvin Karpis was eventually captured in 1936 and sentenced to life in prison, where he served time until his release on parole in 1969. The other gang members were either killed, captured, or faded into obscurity. The legacy of Ma Barker and the Barker-Karpis gang, however, lived on in the public imagination.

The portrayal of Ma Barker in popular culture has been diverse and often sensationalized. She has been depicted in numerous films, books, and television shows, usually as a larger-than-life figure who embodied the lawlessness and rebellious spirit of the Depression-era gangster culture. Movies such as "Ma Barker's Killer Brood" (1960) and "Bloody Mama" (1970) portrayed her as a ruthless and controlling matriarch who led her sons into a life of crime. These depictions, while entertaining, often took significant liberties with the historical record, blending fact and fiction to create a compelling narrative.

Ma Barker's story is emblematic of the broader social and economic conditions of the time. The Great Depression created an environment of widespread poverty and desperation, conditions that contributed to the rise of organized crime as a means of survival and resistance. The Barker family's descent into crime can be seen as a microcosm of the struggles faced by many American families during this period. Their story reflects the broader themes of economic hardship, social instability, and the allure of criminality as a means of escaping poverty and achieving a semblance of power and control.

In recent years, historians and scholars have continued to reexamine the life and legacy of Ma Barker, seeking to separate the myths from the realities. This ongoing research has provided a more nuanced understanding of her role in the Barker-Karpis gang and the dynamics of the family. While the legend of Ma Barker as a criminal mastermind persists, the historical evidence suggests a more complex and multifaceted character. She was a mother who, despite her flaws and failings, sought to provide for and protect her sons in a world that offered few opportunities for people of their social standing.

The legacy of Ma Barker remains a compelling chapter in the history of American crime, a story that continues to captivate and intrigue. Her life, marked by poverty, familial loyalty, and association with some of the most notorious criminals of the era, offers valuable insights into the social and economic conditions that shaped the criminal underworld of the early 20th century. As historians continue to uncover new details and reassess old narratives, the story of Ma Barker and the Barker-Karpis gang will undoubtedly continue to evolve, providing a deeper understanding of this fascinating and enigmatic figure.

Chapter 10: Pancho Villa

Pancho Villa, born José Doroteo Arango Arámbula on June 5, 1878, in the state of Durango, Mexico, is one of the most iconic and complex figures in Mexican history. His life story is a tapestry of revolutionary zeal, charismatic leadership, ruthless tactics, and enduring controversy. Villa's role in the Mexican Revolution of the early 20th century cemented his status as both a folk hero and a contentious symbol of social upheaval and change.

Villa's early life was marked by hardship and poverty. Born to a poor peasant family, he experienced the brutal realities of rural life in Porfirio Díaz's Mexico, a period characterized by stark economic inequality and social stratification. After his father's death, young José Doroteo assumed responsibility for his family. According to popular legend, he adopted the alias "Francisco Villa" (later shortened to Pancho Villa) after killing a local hacienda owner who had assaulted his sister, although some historians debate the accuracy of this account. Regardless, this incident marked his entry into a life of banditry and rebellion.

Villa's transformation from a bandit into a revolutionary leader began with his deepening resentment towards the entrenched social injustices perpetuated by the Díaz regime. Díaz's long-standing dictatorship was marked by favoritism towards the wealthy landowners and foreign interests, while the majority of Mexicans, especially the indigenous and mestizo populations, lived in abject poverty. Villa's early acts of banditry, targeting wealthy landowners and distributing loot among the poor, earned him a Robin Hood-like reputation. This image of a social bandit laid the groundwork for his later role as a revolutionary.

The Mexican Revolution, which erupted in 1910, was a complex and multifaceted conflict driven by a diverse array of social, political, and economic grievances. Villa emerged as a key figure in the revolution's early stages, aligning himself with Francisco I. Madero, a wealthy landowner who advocated for democratic reforms and the end of Díaz's dictatorship. Villa's military prowess and ability to mobilize peasant support made him an invaluable ally to Madero. Together, they contributed to the ousting of Díaz in 1911, marking the end of a 35-year dictatorship and a significant turning point in Mexican history.

However, the revolution did not end with Díaz's departure. The power vacuum and differing visions for Mexico's future led to further conflicts. Madero's presidency faced opposition from various factions, including conservative forces loyal to the old regime and radical revolutionaries who felt that Madero's reforms did not go far enough. In 1913, General Victoriano Huerta orchestrated a coup, assassinating Madero and seizing power. This betrayal reignited the revolutionary fervor, and Villa became one of the key leaders in the struggle against Huerta's dictatorship.

As the commander of the División del Norte (Division of the North), Villa demonstrated extraordinary military acumen. His strategies, often unorthodox and innovative, led to a series of significant victories against Huerta's forces. Villa's ability to inspire loyalty among his troops, many of whom were fellow peasants, was a crucial factor in his success. He fostered a sense of camaraderie and shared purpose, often participating in battles alongside his men and ensuring they were well-provisioned and motivated. His leadership style, characterized by a combination of charisma, discipline, and populist rhetoric, endeared him to his followers and established him as a formidable revolutionary leader.

Villa's success on the battlefield was paralleled by his efforts to implement social and economic reforms in the territories he controlled. He sought to address some of the fundamental grievances that had fueled the revolution, including land redistribution and workers' rights. Villa's administration in the northern state of Chihuahua, where he had established a stronghold, implemented progressive policies aimed at improving the lives of the local population. He confiscated large estates and redistributed the land to peasants, established schools and hospitals, and regulated prices to prevent exploitation by merchants. These measures, although often implemented with a heavy hand, reflected his commitment to social justice and his vision of a more equitable society.

Villa's alliance with Venustiano Carranza, another prominent revolutionary leader, was a marriage of convenience aimed at ousting Huerta. However, their differing visions for Mexico's future soon led to conflict. Carranza, who favored a more centralized and conservative approach to governance, clashed with Villa's radical and populist ideals. The fragile alliance fractured, and by 1914, Villa and Carranza were in open conflict. This period of the revolution, often referred to as the "Civil War within the Revolution," saw Villa pitted against Carranza's forces in a brutal struggle for supremacy.

The rivalry between Villa and Carranza culminated in the Battle of Celaya in 1915, one of the largest and bloodiest battles of the Mexican Revolution. Villa's forces suffered a devastating defeat at the hands of General Álvaro Obregón, Carranza's most skilled commander. Obregón's use of modern military tactics, including trench warfare and barbed wire, proved decisive. Villa's reliance on traditional cavalry charges and his underestimation of Obregón's strategic capabilities contributed to his defeat. The loss at Celaya marked a turning point in Villa's fortunes, and his forces were gradually pushed back into the northern regions of Mexico.

Despite his military setbacks, Villa's reputation as a tenacious and resilient leader remained intact. He continued to wage a guerrilla war against Carranza's forces, utilizing his knowledge of the rugged terrain of northern Mexico to conduct hit-and-run attacks. Villa's ability to evade capture and his persistence in the face of adversity endeared him to many Mexicans, who viewed him as a symbol of resistance against oppression.

In 1916, Villa's actions took on an international dimension when he led a raid on the town of Columbus, New Mexico. The raid, which resulted in the deaths of several Americans and the destruction of property, was a bold and provocative act intended to draw the United States into the conflict. Villa hoped that American intervention would destabilize Carranza's regime and create an opportunity for his own resurgence. In response, President Woodrow Wilson authorized the Punitive Expedition, led by General John J. Pershing, to capture Villa. The expedition, which involved thousands of U.S. troops, failed to achieve its objective, as Villa skillfully evaded capture. The incursion into Mexican territory, however, strained relations between the United States and Mexico and highlighted the complexities of the revolution.

As the revolution wore on, Villa's influence waned. The rise of Obregón and the consolidation of Carranza's power marginalized Villa's role in the broader revolutionary movement. By 1920, Carranza's regime was itself overthrown, and Obregón assumed the presidency. Recognizing the futility of continued resistance, Villa negotiated an amnesty with Obregón, agreeing to retire from active rebellion in exchange for a large hacienda in Chihuahua and a modest stipend.

Villa's retirement from public life did not diminish his legendary status. He settled at the Hacienda de Canutillo, where he attempted to lead a quieter life, surrounded by his family and a small group of loyal followers. However, his past could not be entirely escaped. Villa remained a figure of fascination and fear, with many viewing him as a potential threat to the new political order. On July 20, 1923, Villa was assassinated in an ambush near his ranch. The circumstances surrounding his death remain a subject of speculation and conspiracy theories, with various factions and individuals potentially having motives for eliminating him.

Pancho Villa's legacy is a tapestry of heroism, controversy, and enduring fascination. He is celebrated as a champion of the poor and a symbol of resistance against tyranny. His actions and leadership during the Mexican Revolution had a profound impact on the course of Mexican history, contributing to the eventual overthrow of the Díaz regime and the establishment of a more democratic government. Villa's commitment to social justice and his efforts to address the inequalities that plagued Mexican society resonated with many, solidifying his status as a folk hero.

However, Villa's legacy is also marked by violence and ruthlessness. His military campaigns often involved brutal tactics, including executions and reprisals against those who opposed him. The raid on Columbus, New Mexico, and other acts of violence against civilians complicate the narrative of Villa as a purely heroic figure. His methods and the chaos that accompanied his actions reflect the broader complexities and moral ambiguities of the Mexican Revolution.

In popular culture, Villa has been depicted in numerous films, books, and songs, each interpretation adding to the mythos surrounding him. The 1968 film "Villa Rides," starring Yul Brynner, and the 2003 miniseries "And Starring Pancho Villa as Himself," featuring Antonio Banderas, are just a few examples of how Villa's story has been adapted for the screen. These portrayals, while often dramatized, capture the essence of Villa's larger-than-life personality and his impact on Mexican and world history.

Scholarly interest in Villa continues to yield new insights into his life and the broader context of the Mexican Revolution. Historians have examined his military strategies, leadership style, and the social and economic conditions that fueled his rise to prominence. Villa's interactions with other revolutionary leaders, his relationships with foreign powers, and his vision for Mexico's future are subjects of ongoing research and debate.

Pancho Villa's story is a microcosm of the Mexican Revolution's broader themes of social justice, resistance, and the struggle for a better future. His life, marked by both extraordinary achievements and profound controversies, embodies the complexities of revolutionary change. As Mexico and the world continue to grapple with issues of inequality, power, and resistance, Villa's legacy serves as a reminder of the enduring impact of one man's quest to reshape his society.

43

Chapter 11: Jack Sheppard

Jack Sheppard, one of the most infamous and celebrated thieves in English history, was born in the impoverished district of Spitalfields in London in 1702. His early life was steeped in hardship and destitution. His father, a carpenter, passed away when Jack was young, leaving the family in a precarious situation. Despite these adverse conditions, Jack's mother managed to secure an apprenticeship for him with a carpenter named Owen Wood. This apprenticeship was meant to set Jack on a path to a stable and respectable profession. However, life had other plans for him.

Sheppard quickly became disillusioned with the hard, honest labor of carpentry. He found the monotony and physical toil unappealing and began to look for more thrilling and lucrative ways to make a living. His natural charm, good looks, and roguish demeanor made him popular among his peers, and he soon found himself drawn into the world of petty crime. It was in this underworld of thieves, prostitutes, and gamblers that Sheppard's true talents began to shine.

His criminal career began with small thefts and burglaries, but it wasn't long before his activities escalated. His first major brush with the law came in 1723, when he was arrested for theft and imprisoned in St. Giles's Roundhouse, a notorious local jail. Remarkably, Sheppard managed to escape within a few hours by breaking through the roof. This feat was the first of many daring escapes that would make him famous. Over the next year, Sheppard's life became a series of arrests and escapes, each more audacious than the last.

Sheppard's most famous escape occurred in October 1724, when he was incarcerated in Newgate Prison, one of the most secure and feared prisons in London. Locked in a high-security cell, heavily chained, and under constant surveillance, it seemed impossible for him to break free. However, Sheppard's ingenuity and determination were unmatched. Using a piece of metal, he managed to pick the locks on his chains. He then broke through a series of iron bars and wooden barriers, ultimately scaling the prison's roof. From there, he climbed down into the yard and made his way to freedom, despite the considerable height and danger involved. This escape, often referred to as his "great escape," cemented his reputation as an extraordinary escape artist and a folk hero.

The public was fascinated by Sheppard's ability to outwit the authorities and break free from seemingly impregnable prisons. His exploits were widely reported in newspapers and pamphlets, and he became a symbol of defiance against the harsh and often corrupt justice system of the time. People saw in Sheppard a rebellious spirit who refused to be crushed by the oppressive forces of society. His story resonated particularly with the poor and disenfranchised, who admired his audacity and cunning.

However, Sheppard's luck could not hold out forever. After his final escape from Newgate, he was recaptured just a few weeks later. Exhausted and weakened by the constant pressure of being on the run, he was unable to evade capture. This time, the authorities took no chances. He was placed in even more secure confinement, under heavy guard and constant watch. Despite public sympathy and petitions for clemency, the authorities were determined to make an example of him.

On November 16, 1724, Jack Sheppard was executed by hanging at Tyburn, a fate that was almost inevitable given his high-profile criminal career. His execution was a major public event, attended by thousands who came to witness the end of the legendary escape artist. Even in death, Sheppard's influence was profound. His life story continued to be told and retold in ballads, plays, and pamphlets for many years, keeping his memory alive in the public consciousness.

Sheppard's legacy endures as a fascinating blend of criminality and heroism. He was undoubtedly a thief and a lawbreaker, yet his charm, ingenuity, and defiance against a harsh and often corrupt legal system won him a unique place in history. His life raises questions about the nature of crime, punishment, and the human spirit's unyielding desire for freedom. In many ways, Sheppard's story reflects broader societal issues of his time, including the stark inequalities and the harshness of the penal system. His ability to capture the public's imagination speaks to a deep-seated admiration for those who dare to challenge authority and seek liberation, even through unlawful means.

Jack Sheppard's tale is a compelling narrative of audacity, skill, and the timeless allure of the underdog. His escapes from prison were not just physical acts of breaking free but symbolized a deeper yearning for autonomy and self-determination. Despite his criminal actions, Sheppard's legacy as a folk hero highlights the complexities of societal values and the enduring fascination with those who live outside the law. His story, steeped in both historical reality and mythic embellishment, continues to resonate as a testament to the human spirit's capacity for resilience and rebellion.

Chapter 12: Black Bart

Black Bart, born Charles Earl Bowles around 1829 in Norfolk, England, is one of the most enigmatic and notorious figures in the history of the American West. His life story is a fascinating tale of transformation from an English immigrant to a feared and respected highwayman, famous for his poetic flair and gentlemanly demeanor. Bowles' early life was marked by the typical hardships faced by immigrants in the 19th century. His family relocated to Jefferson County, New York, when he was just two years old, seeking better opportunities in the New World.

As a young man, Bowles was drawn to the promise of wealth and adventure that characterized the California Gold Rush. In 1849, he and his brothers journeyed to California, where they tried their luck at gold mining. The endeavor proved challenging, and while there were occasional successes, the harsh realities of mining life took their toll. Bowles experienced firsthand the struggles and frustrations that many miners faced, and these experiences likely shaped his later actions.

By 1854, disillusioned with mining and seeking new prospects, Bowles returned east and married Mary Elizabeth Johnson. The couple settled in Decatur, Illinois, where they started a family. However, Bowles' restless spirit soon led him back to the West. He joined the Union Army during the Civil War, serving with distinction in the 116th Illinois Regiment. His military service, which included participation in major battles such as Vicksburg, provided him with valuable skills and a sense of discipline that would later aid his criminal career.

After the war, Bowles briefly returned to family life but was once again drawn to the West, this time as a means of escape from his domestic responsibilities and financial difficulties. By the late 1860s, he had vanished from the records, reemerging in the early 1870s as Black Bart, a name that would soon become legendary.

Black Bart's career as a stagecoach robber began in 1875, targeting Wells Fargo stagecoaches in Northern California and Southern Oregon. Unlike many of his contemporaries, Bart conducted his robberies with a remarkable degree of sophistication and politeness. He became known for his distinctive style, which included wearing a linen duster, a bowler hat, and a flour sack with eye holes over his head. This attire not only disguised his identity but also added an element of drama to his exploits.

Bart's modus operandi was as unique as his appearance. He operated alone, without the violent confrontations typical of other outlaws of his time. Armed with a shotgun, which he never fired, Bart would calmly demand the strongbox and any valuables the passengers carried. His demeanor during these hold-ups was consistently described as courteous and gentlemanly, often reassuring his victims that he meant them no harm. This approach earned him a measure of respect and even a peculiar kind of admiration from those he robbed.

One of the most intriguing aspects of Black Bart's robberies was his penchant for leaving behind poetic messages. These poems, often signed "Black Bart, the Po8," added a literary flair to his criminal activities and contributed to his mystique. His verses, while not particularly sophisticated, were a clear indication of his desire to be remembered as more than just a common thief. One of his most famous poems, left at the scene of an 1877 robbery, read:

"I've labored long and hard for bread, for honor, and for riches, but on my corns too long you've trodden, You fine-haired sons of bitches."

These poetic notes fascinated the public and the press, turning Black Bart into a folk hero of sorts. His ability to elude capture for so long only added to his legend. Bart's success can be attributed to his careful planning, intimate knowledge of the rugged terrain, and the element of surprise. He struck remote and isolated stagecoach routes, timing his heists to maximize the chances of success and minimize the risk of apprehension.

Despite his cunning and careful planning, Black Bart's criminal career eventually came to an end. His downfall began with a robbery in 1883, during which he made a rare mistake. After holding up a stagecoach in Calaveras County, Bart left behind a handkerchief with a laundry mark, leading investigators to a laundromat in San Francisco. This clue eventually led Wells Fargo detectives to Charles E. Boles, a quiet, respectable man living in a modest boarding house. Under intense scrutiny and pressure, Boles confessed to being Black Bart but maintained his gentlemanly composure even in custody.

Bart's trial was a sensation, drawing significant public attention. He was sentenced to six years in San Quentin State Prison. During his incarceration, Bart remained a model prisoner, earning the respect of both inmates and guards. His gentlemanly demeanor and adherence to a personal code of conduct continued to set him apart from other criminals.

Upon his release in 1888, Black Bart disappeared from public view. There are numerous theories about what happened to him after his release. Some suggest he moved to Montana or Nevada to live out his remaining years in obscurity, while others believe he returned to his family under a new identity. Despite extensive searches and speculation, the final chapter of Black Bart's life remains shrouded in mystery, adding another layer to his enigmatic legacy.

Black Bart's story is a compelling narrative of transformation, ingenuity, and the human desire for recognition and respect, even in the most unlikely of professions. His life as a stagecoach robber stands out not only because of his unique methods and poetic inclinations but also because of the way he has been romanticized in American folklore. Unlike many outlaws of the Old West, Bart's legacy is one of wit over violence, and style over brutality. His courteous demeanor, combined with his literary attempts, created an image of a cultured rogue, a far cry from the brutal and ruthless criminals of his time.

In essence, Black Bart's life and legend offer a glimpse into the complexities of human character and the myriad ways individuals seek to carve out their place in history. His story is a reminder that even in a world as harsh and unforgiving as the American West, there is room for nuance, creativity, and the unexpected. The legend of Black Bart endures because it defies the simple categorization of good and evil, presenting instead a portrait of a man who, while undeniably a criminal, possessed a distinct sense of style, honor, and a touch of poetic soul.

Chapter 13: Bartolomeo Vanzetti and Nicola Sacco

Bartolomeo Vanzetti and Nicola Sacco were two Italian immigrants whose lives became inextricably linked in one of the most famous and controversial legal cases in American history. Their story, filled with themes of injustice, xenophobia, and political turmoil, captures a pivotal moment in the early 20th century when the United States grappled with issues of immigration, labor rights, and radical political movements.

Bartolomeo Vanzetti was born on June 11, 1888, in Villafalletto, Italy, into a poor farming family. Despite showing early academic promise, he had to leave school at the age of thirteen to work and support his family. This hardship instilled in him a strong sense of social justice and a deep empathy for the working class. Vanzetti immigrated to the United States in 1908, seeking better economic opportunities. However, the reality of immigrant life in America was harsh, and he found himself working various low-paying, menial jobs. Despite these challenges, Vanzetti educated himself, becoming a passionate advocate for workers' rights and anarchism.

Nicola Sacco, born on April 22, 1891, in Torremaggiore, Italy, also came from a modest background. Like Vanzetti, he emigrated to the United States in search of a better life, arriving in 1908. Sacco settled in Massachusetts, where he worked as a skilled shoemaker. He too became involved in the labor movement and was an ardent supporter of anarchism, influenced by the writings of Luigi Galleani, an Italian anarchist whose radical ideas called for the overthrow of the capitalist system through direct action, including violence if necessary.

The lives of Sacco and Vanzetti intersected in the early 1910s through their mutual involvement in anarchist circles. Both men were deeply committed to the cause, attending meetings, participating in strikes, and distributing radical literature. The political climate of the time was charged with fear and suspicion, particularly toward immigrants and those associated with leftist ideologies. The Russian Revolution of 1917 and subsequent Red Scare heightened these tensions, leading to widespread anti-immigrant sentiment and a crackdown on radical political activities.

On April 15, 1920, a crime occurred that would thrust Sacco and Vanzetti into the national spotlight. In South Braintree, Massachusetts, a payroll robbery resulted in the deaths of two men: Alessandro Berardelli, a security guard, and Frederick Parmenter, a paymaster. The assailants escaped with more than $15,000, leaving few clues behind. The police, under intense pressure to solve the case, focused their attention on local anarchists, leading to the arrests of Sacco and Vanzetti on May 5, 1920.

The evidence against Sacco and Vanzetti was circumstantial and controversial from the outset. Sacco was carrying a gun when arrested, and both men were found with anarchist literature, which the prosecution used to paint them as dangerous radicals. Witnesses provided conflicting testimonies, with some identifying the two men as the robbers while others could not. The ballistics evidence, which later became a focal point of debate, was inconclusive. The prosecution argued that a bullet found at the crime scene matched Sacco's gun, but experts disagreed on the reliability of this match.

The trial, held in Dedham, Massachusetts, in 1921, was highly publicized and widely regarded as biased. The presiding judge, Webster Thayer, was openly hostile to the defendants, referring to them derogatorily and making prejudiced comments. The prosecution's case leaned heavily on the defendants' political beliefs and immigrant status, rather than solid evidence linking them to the crime. Despite these issues, Sacco and Vanzetti were found guilty on July 14, 1921, and sentenced to death.

The verdict sparked international outrage and a massive public outcry. Intellectuals, writers, and activists from around the world rallied to the cause, arguing that Sacco and Vanzetti were being persecuted for their political beliefs rather than for any concrete evidence of their guilt. Notable figures such as Albert Einstein, H.G. Wells, and Dorothy Parker spoke out against the conviction. Protests and demonstrations were held in major cities across the globe, and numerous appeals and motions for a new trial were filed, citing judicial bias and new evidence.

Despite these efforts, the appeals were consistently denied. The case dragged on for seven years, during which time Sacco and Vanzetti remained imprisoned. Their letters from prison revealed their unwavering belief in their innocence and their commitment to the anarchist cause. They became symbols of the broader struggle against injustice and the oppressive forces of the state.

In a final effort to save their lives, supporters presented new evidence and affidavits from witnesses who claimed others had confessed to the crime. One of the most significant pieces of new evidence came from Celestino Madeiros, a convicted murderer, who confessed to being part of the South Braintree robbery and exonerated Sacco and Vanzetti. However, the courts dismissed Madeiros' confession as unreliable and refused to grant a new trial.

On August 23, 1927, despite worldwide protests and last-minute attempts to stay their execution, Nicola Sacco and Bartolomeo Vanzetti were executed in the electric chair at Charlestown State Prison. Their deaths were met with immediate and widespread condemnation. Vigils and riots erupted in cities around the world, and their funeral procession in Boston drew tens of thousands of mourners.

The legacy of Sacco and Vanzetti endures as a powerful symbol of the perils of prejudice and the miscarriages of justice that can occur when fear and xenophobia are allowed to influence the legal system. In the decades following their execution, efforts to clear their names continued. In 1977, on the 50th anniversary of their deaths, Massachusetts Governor Michael Dukakis issued a proclamation stating that Sacco and Vanzetti had been unfairly tried and convicted, and that "any disgrace should be forever removed from their names."

The case of Sacco and Vanzetti remains a poignant reminder of the dangers faced by those who challenge the status quo and the importance of safeguarding civil liberties and the principles of justice. Their story has been immortalized in literature, film, and music, serving as a testament to their enduring impact on American society and the ongoing struggle for justice and equality.

Sacco and Vanzetti's story continues to resonate today as a cautionary tale about the consequences of a legal system influenced by political and social prejudices. It highlights the importance of due process, impartiality in the judiciary, and the protection of individual rights against the backdrop of broader societal fears and biases. Their case also underscores the role of public opinion and activism in challenging injustices and advocating for the wrongfully accused.

Chapter 14: Charles Peace

Charles Peace, one of England's most notorious criminals of the 19th century, lived a life that epitomized the dark and dangerous underbelly of Victorian society. Born on May 14, 1832, in Darnall, Sheffield, his early life was steeped in hardship and poverty. His father, John Peace, was a shoemaker and later a nail maker, struggling to support his family on meager earnings. The young Charles Peace did not have the benefit of a stable and nurturing environment, and his formative years were marked by physical disabilities and neglect. At a young age, he suffered a severe accident at a steel mill, which left him with a permanent limp and a deformed leg. This injury not only caused him physical pain but also limited his opportunities for regular employment.

Peace's early brush with crime came as a consequence of his challenging circumstances. In his teenage years, he began to dabble in petty theft, driven by the harsh realities of his environment and a need to survive. His initial forays into criminal activity were minor, but they set the stage for a career that would soon escalate in both ambition and notoriety. By the time he was in his twenties, Peace had already served time in prison for burglary. His time behind bars, rather than reforming him, seemed to reinforce his criminal tendencies and introduced him to more experienced criminals who would influence his future exploits.

The 1860s saw Peace transition from petty theft to more serious crimes. He became an accomplished burglar, known for his cunning and skill in evading capture. His burglaries were characterized by meticulous planning and a deep knowledge of the urban landscapes in which he operated. Peace's ability to scout out wealthy homes and his use of innovative techniques to gain entry without detection made him a master of his illicit trade. He frequently targeted affluent neighborhoods, including areas in Manchester, Liverpool, and

Sheffield. His activities during this period earned him a reputation as one of the most elusive burglars in England.

Peace's criminal career took a darker turn in the 1870s with the escalation of his violent tendencies. In 1876, he committed the crime that would ultimately lead to his downfall. Peace had become infatuated with a woman named Mrs. Hannah Dyson, who was married to a civil engineer named Arthur Dyson. Despite being married himself, Peace pursued Mrs. Dyson obsessively. When she rebuffed his advances, Peace's response was chillingly violent. On November 29, 1876, Peace shot and killed Arthur Dyson as he was returning home from work. This cold-blooded murder marked a significant escalation in Peace's criminal activities and set off a manhunt that would eventually lead to his capture.

After the murder of Arthur Dyson, Peace fled to London, where he assumed a new identity as John Ward, a gentleman of means. This period of his life was marked by a remarkable transformation as Peace attempted to distance himself from his criminal past. He rented a house in Peckham and lived a seemingly respectable life, mingling with society and even marrying again. Despite his attempts to lead a quiet life, Peace could not resist the lure of burglary. He continued to commit high-profile burglaries, maintaining his reputation as an elusive and daring criminal.

The law eventually caught up with Peace in 1878, after a bungled burglary in Blackheath, London. During the attempted burglary, Peace shot at but only wounded a police officer named Constable Robinson, who was investigating suspicious activity in the area. Despite being injured, the officer managed to alert his colleagues, leading to Peace's arrest. The subsequent investigation revealed his true identity and his connection to the murder of Arthur Dyson. Peace's trial for the murder was held in Leeds in February 1879, and the evidence against him was overwhelming. Eyewitness testimony, forensic evidence, and Peace's own incriminating statements during his interrogation sealed his fate. He was found guilty and sentenced to death.

Charles Peace's execution took place on February 25, 1879, at Armley Gaol in Leeds. His death marked the end of a criminal career that had spanned decades and left a lasting impact on Victorian society. Peace's notoriety was such that his life and crimes were extensively covered in the press, turning him into a figure of public fascination and revulsion. His story was further immortalized in various forms of popular culture, including ballads, plays, and later, films. The sensational nature of his crimes, combined with his complex personality, made Peace a compelling figure whose legacy endured long after his death.

One of the most intriguing aspects of Charles Peace's life was his dual nature. On one hand, he was a ruthless criminal capable of committing cold-blooded murder without remorse. On the other hand, he was a man of considerable charm and intelligence, able to assume different identities and blend into respectable society. This duality made him a particularly dangerous and elusive criminal, as he was able to exploit the trust and goodwill of those around him to further his criminal activities.

Peace's ability to evade capture for so long can be attributed to several factors. His meticulous planning and execution of burglaries, combined with his knowledge of urban environments, allowed him to stay one step ahead of the law. He also maintained a network of criminal associates who provided him with information and support. Additionally, Peace's charm and ability to assume different personas helped him to avoid suspicion and blend into different communities.

The legacy of Charles Peace is a complex one. While he is remembered primarily as a notorious criminal, his life also sheds light on the broader social and economic conditions of Victorian England. Peace's criminal activities were, in part, a response to the harsh realities of life for many working-class individuals during this period. The lack of economic opportunities, combined with the social stigma attached to disability, played a significant role in shaping his life choices.

Chapter 15: Dick Turpin

Richard "Dick" Turpin, an iconic figure in British folklore, has been romanticized as a dashing highwayman, but his true-life story is far grittier and more complex. Born on September 21, 1705, in Hempstead, Essex, Turpin's early life gave little indication of the infamy he would later achieve. He was the son of a butcher, John Turpin, and learned the trade from his father. However, the lure of a more adventurous and lucrative life led him away from the butchery and into a life of crime.

Turpin's criminal career began in the early 1730s. Initially, he joined a gang of deer thieves led by the notorious Thomas Easter. Poaching was a common crime at the time, and Turpin's involvement in it was a stepping stone to more serious offenses. The gang operated in Epping Forest, a large wooded area near London, where they would steal livestock and game. This period of his life honed Turpin's skills in stealth, horsemanship, and the art of evading capture, which would serve him well in his later exploits.

As the authorities cracked down on poaching, Turpin and his gang shifted their focus to burglary. They began targeting isolated farmhouses and rural homes, employing brutal tactics to intimidate and rob their victims. One of their most infamous crimes was the attack on the house of a farmer named Joseph Lawrence. The gang tortured Lawrence's elderly servant, with Turpin allegedly holding her over a fire to force her to reveal the location of hidden valuables. Such violent and ruthless methods characterized Turpin's approach to crime, contrasting sharply with the later romanticized image of him as a gallant highwayman.

The gang's activities soon drew the attention of the authorities, leading to the capture and execution of several members. Turpin managed to evade capture and went into hiding. It was during this time that he began to reinvent himself as a highwayman. The term "highwayman" referred to robbers who preyed on travelers along the nation's roads, often on horseback, and Turpin quickly gained notoriety in this new role.

By the mid-1730s, Turpin had established himself as one of the most feared highwaymen in England. His daring exploits on the highways around London, particularly on the Great North Road, made him a household name. Unlike his earlier crimes, Turpin's highway robberies were marked by a certain panache. He would often dress in fine clothes, sometimes even in disguise, and his audacious methods of stopping carriages and demanding money from their occupants became legendary. One of his most famous exploits was the robbery of a group of travelers near Epping Forest, where he allegedly took on multiple armed guards single-handedly, a feat that contributed to his growing mythos.

Turpin's fame as a highwayman was further cemented by his association with another notorious figure, Tom King, also known as "The Gentleman Highwayman." King was known for his charm and politeness, which provided a stark contrast to Turpin's brutality. Together, they formed a formidable duo, carrying out a series of high-profile robberies that captured the public's imagination. Their partnership, however, was short-lived. In 1737, during an attempted arrest, Turpin accidentally shot and killed King, which forced him to flee and marked the beginning of the end for his criminal career.

Following King's death, Turpin's life took a downward spiral. He continued his criminal activities but found it increasingly difficult to evade capture. The net was closing in on him as the authorities intensified their efforts to bring him to justice. In the summer of 1737, Turpin stole several horses and fled to the northern counties of England, assuming the alias John Palmer. He tried to blend into rural communities, passing himself off as a gentleman horse trader. However, his arrogant and often violent behavior soon aroused suspicion.

Turpin's downfall began in the small village of Brough, in the East Riding of Yorkshire. His habit of poaching and stealing livestock led to his arrest in October 1738 for shooting a neighbor's cockerel and threatening local residents. While in custody, Turpin boasted of his exploits and wrote a letter to his brother-in-law, seeking assistance. The letter, however, was intercepted, and Turpin's true identity was revealed when his old schoolmaster, James Smith, recognized his handwriting. This recognition led to Turpin being charged with horse theft, a capital offense at the time.

Turpin's trial took place at York Assizes in March 1739. Despite his notoriety, he received a fair trial by the standards of the day. Witnesses testified to his various crimes, and the evidence against him was overwhelming. On March 22, 1739, Turpin was found guilty of horse theft and sentenced to death. His execution took place on April 7, 1739, at Knavesmire, the common execution site in York. Turpin faced his death with notable bravado, reportedly bowing to the spectators and even hiring five men to act as mourners at his funeral.

The legend of Dick Turpin was largely shaped by popular culture in the years following his death. The romanticized version of Turpin as a dashing and chivalrous highwayman emerged in the early 19th century, most notably in William Harrison Ainsworth's novel "Rookwood," published in 1834. Ainsworth's depiction of Turpin's mythical ride from London to York on his loyal steed, Black Bess, cemented his place in folklore. This legendary ride, supposedly covering over 200 miles in a single night to establish an alibi for a crime, was pure fiction but contributed significantly to the enduring myth of Dick Turpin.

Turpin's transformation from a violent criminal to a folk hero reflects broader societal changes and the romanticization of the past. The public's fascination with highwaymen, who were seen as rebels against the established order, captured the imagination of a society undergoing rapid industrialization and social upheaval. Turpin, in particular, embodied the contradictory qualities of violence and charm, which made him a compelling figure in popular culture.

In examining the true life of Dick Turpin, it becomes evident that he was far from the noble outlaw of legend. His crimes were marked by brutality and a disregard for human life, driven by a desire for wealth and notoriety. The romanticized image of Turpin as a gallant rogue serves as a reminder of how history can be shaped and reshaped by storytelling, often glossing over the harsher realities in favor of a more appealing narrative.

Turpin's enduring legacy is a testament to the power of myth and the human fascination with outlaws who defy authority. While the real Dick Turpin was a far cry from the hero of folklore, his story continues to capture the public's imagination, serving as a symbol of rebellion and adventure in a world that has long since left the era of highwaymen behind. His life, marked by crime and violence, contrasts sharply with the legendary figure who gallops through the annals of English history, a testament to the enduring allure of the outlaw and the power of storytelling in shaping our understanding of the past.

Chapter 16: Jesse James

Jesse James, an American outlaw whose life and exploits have become the stuff of legend, embodies the tumultuous period of post-Civil War America. Born on September 5, 1847, in Kearney, Missouri, Jesse Woodson James grew up in a world defined by violence and conflict. His father, Robert James, was a Baptist minister who left home to join the California Gold Rush, leaving behind a young Jesse, his brother Frank, and their mother, Zerelda James. The family's fortunes declined after Robert's death, leading Zerelda to remarry multiple times. This instability, combined with the volatile political climate of the time, deeply influenced the young Jesse James.

The American Civil War, which broke out in 1861, profoundly affected Jesse and his older brother Frank. Missouri was a border state with divided loyalties, and the James brothers sided with the Confederacy. Frank James joined the pro-Confederate guerrilla group led by William Clarke Quantrill, known as Quantrill's Raiders, infamous for their brutal tactics and hit-and-run operations. Jesse, though younger, soon followed suit. By 1864, he had joined the bushwhacker group led by "Bloody Bill" Anderson, participating in violent raids that targeted Union sympathizers. These experiences hardened Jesse, instilling in him a taste for violence and a deep-seated resentment towards the Union.

After the war, Jesse and Frank found it difficult to return to normal life. Missouri was a hotbed of resentment and economic hardship, particularly for former Confederates. The Reconstruction era saw the imposition of harsh measures on the South, exacerbating tensions. In this environment, the James brothers transitioned from guerrilla warfare to a life of crime. They joined or formed various gangs, including the James-Younger Gang, partnering with fellow ex-Confederates such as Cole Younger. Their criminal activities began with small-time robberies but quickly escalated.

The first major crime attributed to Jesse James was the robbery of the Clay County Savings Association in Liberty, Missouri, on February 13, 1866. The gang made off with a significant sum of money, and the robbery resulted in the death of a bystander, a chilling foreshadowing of the violent career that lay ahead. This marked the beginning of a spree of bank and train robberies that would make Jesse James a household name. Over the next decade, the James-Younger Gang became notorious for their daring heists and violent methods.

One of their most famous robberies occurred on July 21, 1873, when the gang derailed a train near Adair, Iowa, and looted its safe. This event cemented Jesse James's reputation as a fearless and audacious outlaw. Train robberies were particularly sensational and captured the public's imagination, partly because they disrupted the symbols of progress and industry. The gang's ability to execute such high-profile crimes while evading capture only added to their mystique.

Jesse James's personal life was as tumultuous as his criminal career. In 1874, he married his first cousin, Zerelda Mimms, named after his mother. They had two children, Jesse Edwards James and Mary James. Despite his life of crime, Jesse attempted to present himself as a devoted family man. However, the constant threat of capture and the need to stay on the move meant that his family life was fraught with danger and instability.

The Pinkerton National Detective Agency, hired by railroad and banking interests, pursued the James-Younger Gang relentlessly. The Pinkertons were known for their aggressive tactics, and the manhunt for Jesse James became a protracted and bloody affair. In 1875, the Pinkertons raided the James family farm, throwing an incendiary device into the house that killed Jesse's half-brother, Archie, and severely injured his mother, Zerelda. This brutal incident only deepened Jesse's resolve to continue his criminal activities and fueled his hatred for the authorities.

The James-Younger Gang's downfall began with a failed bank robbery in Northfield, Minnesota, on September 7, 1876. The citizens of Northfield, alerted to the robbery, fought back, leading to a bloody shootout. Several members of the gang were killed or captured, including the Younger brothers. Jesse and Frank James managed to escape but were now fugitives on the run. This marked a turning point, as the gang never fully recovered its previous strength and cohesion.

In the following years, Jesse James tried to regroup and continue his life of crime, but the pressure from law enforcement and the public was relentless. He formed new gangs and continued to rob banks and trains, but his health and mental state deteriorated. The once fearless outlaw became increasingly paranoid, constantly moving from place to place to avoid capture. His former allies and gang members also began to turn against him, seeking clemency or reward from the authorities.

The end of Jesse James came in St. Joseph, Missouri, on April 3, 1882. Seeking a new life, Jesse had assumed the alias Thomas Howard and was living with his family. He recruited two brothers, Robert and Charley Ford, to join his new gang. Unbeknownst to Jesse, Robert Ford had already made a deal with Missouri Governor Thomas Crittenden to capture or kill Jesse James in exchange for a reward. On that fateful day, as Jesse was dusting a picture on the wall, Robert Ford shot him in the back of the head, killing him instantly. The death of Jesse James at the hands of a fellow outlaw shocked the nation and marked the end of an era.

The legacy of Jesse James is complex and multifaceted. In his lifetime, he was both vilified and celebrated. To many, he was a ruthless criminal whose actions caused untold suffering. To others, especially in the former Confederate states, he was a folk hero, a symbol of resistance against Northern aggression and economic hardship. This duality has persisted in the cultural memory of Jesse James.

The mythologizing of Jesse James began almost immediately after his death. Sensationalized newspaper accounts and dime novels portrayed him as a Robin Hood-like figure, stealing from the rich and giving to the poor. While there is little evidence to support this romanticized view, it resonated with a public eager for heroes and captivated by tales of adventure and rebellion. This image was further perpetuated by Hollywood, with numerous films and television series depicting Jesse James as a charismatic and complex antihero.

Historians, however, paint a more nuanced picture. They acknowledge his role as a product of his time, shaped by the violence and instability of the Civil War and its aftermath. Jesse James's actions were driven by a mix of personal grievances, political beliefs, and sheer opportunism. His story is a reminder of the turbulent period in American history when the lines between hero and villain were often blurred, and the law was frequently a matter of who wielded the most power.

Chapter 17: Billy the Kid

Billy the Kid, born Henry McCarty but also known as William H. Bonney, is one of the most famous outlaws in American history. His life story, a blend of historical fact and mythic legend, captures the lawlessness and tumult of the American Old West. Billy the Kid's short life was marked by his involvement in cattle rustling, numerous escapes from law enforcement, and a series of violent confrontations that would ultimately lead to his death at the age of 21.

Henry McCarty was born on November 23, 1859, in New York City, although some sources suggest he might have been born in Indiana. His parents were Irish immigrants, and after the death of his father, his mother, Catherine McCarty, moved the family west in search of a better life. They eventually settled in Silver City, New Mexico, where Catherine remarried. Young Henry, left largely to his own devices, quickly adapted to the rough-and-tumble life of the frontier.

Henry McCarty's descent into outlawry began with small-time theft. Orphaned by the age of 15 after his mother's death from tuberculosis, he soon found himself in trouble with the law. His first arrest came for stealing food in late 1875, and within a few months, he was arrested again for stealing clothing and firearms. Following this arrest, he escaped from jail, marking the beginning of his life on the run.

Taking on the alias William H. Bonney, Henry drifted through Arizona and New Mexico, falling in with a series of criminal elements. His natural charm and quick wit earned him the nickname "The Kid." By the time he reached his late teens, he had already gained a reputation as a skilled gunfighter. One of his early notable incidents occurred in 1877 when he killed Frank "Windy" Cahill, a blacksmith who had bullied him. The confrontation escalated, and in self-defense, Billy shot Cahill, marking his first known killing.

Billy the Kid's most infamous period began with his involvement in the Lincoln County War, a conflict between rival factions vying for economic control of the county. This violent feud was primarily between the established faction led by James Dolan and Lawrence Murphy, who controlled the local dry goods and cattle market, and a rival group led by John Tunstall and Alexander McSween, who sought to establish their own enterprise. Billy the Kid sided with Tunstall and McSween, who had taken him under their wing, offering him a sense of loyalty and belonging.

The Lincoln County War erupted in February 1878 when Tunstall was murdered by members of the Dolan faction. Tunstall's death deeply affected Billy, who vowed to avenge his friend's murder. He joined a group known as the Regulators, formed to counter the Dolan faction. The Regulators embarked on a campaign of revenge, engaging in several violent confrontations, including the killing of Sheriff William Brady, a Dolan ally. The feud escalated into a series of bloody skirmishes, with both sides suffering casualties.

Billy's role in the Lincoln County War cemented his reputation as a formidable and daring outlaw. He was relentless in his pursuit of justice for Tunstall, and his actions during this period showed his growing confidence and skill as a gunfighter. However, the violence and lawlessness of the conflict also drew the attention of territorial authorities. The Lincoln County War reached its climax in July 1878 with the Battle of Lincoln, a five-day siege involving the Regulators and the Dolan faction. The battle ended with the death of McSween and the dispersal of the Regulators.

Following the end of the Lincoln County War, Billy the Kid continued his life of crime, largely focused on cattle rustling. He and his gang roamed the New Mexico Territory, engaging in sporadic shootouts and clashes with law enforcement. Despite his criminal activities, Billy maintained a certain degree of popular support, especially among those who viewed him as a Robin Hood-like figure resisting the corrupt influences of powerful cattle barons and politicians.

In 1879, New Mexico's newly appointed governor, Lew Wallace, sought to bring order to the territory and offered amnesty to outlaws willing to surrender. Billy the Kid initially expressed interest in the offer and even met with Wallace to negotiate terms. However, the promise of amnesty was never fulfilled, and Billy resumed his criminal activities. His continued defiance of the law made him a target for law enforcement, particularly for Sheriff Pat Garrett, who was determined to capture him.

The relentless pursuit by Garrett and his deputies led to a series of dramatic confrontations. In December 1880, Billy the Kid was captured at Stinking Springs, New Mexico, after a fierce gunfight. He was tried and convicted for the murder of Sheriff Brady during the Lincoln County War and was sentenced to hang. However, Billy's reputation for daring escapes was well-earned. On April 28, 1881, he escaped from the Lincoln County jail, killing two deputies in the process.

Billy the Kid's final months were marked by his status as a fugitive. Sheriff Pat Garrett continued to track him, and on the night of July 14, 1881, Garrett finally caught up with Billy at Fort Sumner, New Mexico. According to Garrett's account, he entered the home of Pete Maxwell, a friend of Billy's, and shot the outlaw in a darkened room, killing him instantly. The death of Billy the Kid at the age of 21 ended the brief but violent career of one of the Old West's most legendary figures.

The legacy of Billy the Kid has been shaped by both historical accounts and mythic narratives. Contemporary newspapers and dime novels sensationalized his exploits, often blurring the lines between fact and fiction. His image as a charming, fearless, and tragic figure has been perpetuated through countless books, films, and songs. While some view him as a ruthless outlaw, others see him as a symbol of youthful rebellion and resistance against a corrupt and oppressive system.

The complexity of Billy the Kid's character lies in his ability to embody the contradictions of the American frontier. He was both a product of and a response to the lawlessness and violence that characterized the post-Civil War West. His life and legend illustrate the harsh realities of frontier justice, where personal vendettas and survival often dictated one's actions. At the same time, the romanticized image of Billy the Kid reflects the enduring fascination with the figure of the outlaw, who challenges authority and lives by his own rules.

Historians have debated the accuracy of many of the stories surrounding Billy the Kid. Some accounts suggest that his kill count was exaggerated, and his role in certain events was embellished to create a more compelling narrative. Regardless of the exact details, there is no doubt that Billy the Kid left a lasting impact on American culture. His story is a reminder of a turbulent period in history when the line between hero and villain was often indistinguishable, and the myths of the Old West were born from the lives of real people who lived and died by the gun.

Chapter 18: Bonnie and Clyde

Bonnie Parker and Clyde Barrow, known simply as Bonnie and Clyde, were a notorious American criminal couple whose violent crime spree during the Great Depression captivated the nation and cemented their place in the annals of American folklore. Their story is one of love, crime, and ultimately tragedy, marked by a series of bank robberies, murders, and dramatic escapes from law enforcement. The legend of Bonnie and Clyde is a testament to the turbulent era of the 1930s, a time when the line between outlaw and folk hero was often blurred.

Bonnie Elizabeth Parker was born on October 1, 1910, in Rowena, Texas. Raised in a poor, working-class family, Bonnie was known for her intelligence and creativity. She excelled in school, particularly in literature and writing, and harbored dreams of becoming a famous actress or poet. However, life had other plans for her. After her father died when she was four, Bonnie's mother moved the family to the Dallas suburb of Cement City. At sixteen, Bonnie married Roy Thornton, but the marriage quickly soured, and Thornton was imprisoned for robbery in 1929. Bonnie never divorced him, though they were estranged by the time she met Clyde Barrow.

Clyde Chestnut Barrow was born on March 24, 1909, into a poor farming family in Ellis County, Texas. Like Bonnie, Clyde grew up in the rough neighborhoods of West Dallas. He was first arrested at the age of 17 for failing to return a rental car, and soon after, he embarked on a life of petty crime. Clyde's criminal activities escalated over time, from stealing cars to committing armed robberies. His initial arrests did little to deter him, and he quickly earned a reputation as a daring and ruthless criminal.

The fateful meeting between Bonnie and Clyde occurred in January 1930 at the home of a mutual friend. The connection between them was immediate and profound, sparking a romance that would drive them both into a life of crime. Shortly after they met, Clyde was arrested for burglary and sentenced to two years in prison. During his incarceration, he was subjected to harsh conditions and brutal treatment, experiences that hardened him and intensified his resolve to rebel against the system. He escaped from prison using a gun that Bonnie had smuggled to him but was recaptured shortly thereafter and sentenced to 14 years of hard labor. He was released in early 1932, thanks to a campaign for his parole led by his mother.

Once Clyde was free, he and Bonnie began their infamous crime spree. Initially, their activities were relatively small-scale, involving a series of gas station and grocery store robberies. However, their crimes soon escalated in both scale and violence. The couple, often accompanied by various accomplices, primarily targeted banks, which were unpopular with many Americans during the Depression due to widespread foreclosures and financial hardships.

Bonnie and Clyde's gang, known as the Barrow Gang, included several members over time, but key figures were Clyde's brother, Marvin "Buck" Barrow, and Buck's wife, Blanche. The gang roamed across the central United States, committing robberies and evading law enforcement through a combination of cunning, speed, and firepower. Clyde, in particular, was known for his driving skills, which were crucial in their numerous escapes.

The gang's first major encounter with law enforcement occurred on April 13, 1933, in Joplin, Missouri. A shootout erupted when police attempted to apprehend them at their hideout. Despite being outgunned, the gang managed to kill two law enforcement officers and escape. The incident marked a significant escalation in their violent confrontations with the police and contributed to their growing notoriety.

As their crime spree continued, the Barrow Gang's exploits were widely reported in the media, turning Bonnie and Clyde into national figures. Newspapers sensationalized their stories, often portraying them as glamorous antiheroes defying a system that many Americans felt had failed them. Photos of Bonnie posing with guns and cigars, discovered after the Joplin shootout, only added to their mythic image. Despite the romanticized portrayal, the reality of their lives was far from glamorous. The gang was constantly on the run, living in stolen cars, cheap motels, and remote hideouts, often in fear for their lives.

The turning point for Bonnie and Clyde came in the summer of 1933 when Buck Barrow was fatally wounded in a shootout with police in Iowa. Blanche Barrow was captured, and the gang was forced to split up. Despite the loss of key members, Bonnie and Clyde continued their criminal activities, but the noose was tightening around them. Law enforcement agencies, led by the Texas Rangers and the FBI, intensified their efforts to capture the notorious couple.

Their final months were marked by a sense of desperation. Injuries sustained in various shootouts, particularly a severe leg injury to Bonnie, hampered their ability to evade capture. They relied on a dwindling circle of accomplices and supporters, but their isolation grew. The public, initially fascinated by their exploits, began to turn against them as the death toll from their crimes rose.

The end came on May 23, 1934, in Bienville Parish, Louisiana. Acting on a tip from a former associate of the gang, a posse of law enforcement officers, led by Texas Ranger Frank Hamer, set an ambush on a rural road. As Bonnie and Clyde drove down the road in their stolen Ford V8, the posse opened fire, riddling the car and its occupants with bullets. The couple died instantly, bringing an abrupt and violent end to their two-year crime spree.

The deaths of Bonnie and Clyde were met with a mix of relief and morbid curiosity. Thousands of people flocked to the scene of their deaths and later to their funerals, eager to get a glimpse of the infamous outlaws. The media coverage further solidified their status as legendary figures of the American West, even as the brutal reality of their actions was laid bare.

The legacy of Bonnie and Clyde has continued to captivate the public imagination. Over the decades, their story has been retold in numerous books, films, and songs, each iteration adding layers to the myth. The 1967 film "Bonnie and Clyde," starring Warren Beatty and Faye Dunaway, played a significant role in shaping the modern perception of the couple as tragic antiheroes. The film's blend of romance, violence, and rebellion resonated with the countercultural sentiments of the 1960s, ensuring that Bonnie and Clyde remained iconic figures.

However, historical accounts provide a more nuanced view of their lives. Far from the glamorous image portrayed in popular culture, Bonnie and Clyde's existence was marked by hardship, violence, and constant fear. Their crimes left a trail of pain and suffering, affecting not only their victims but also their families and the communities they terrorized.

Bonnie Parker, often overshadowed by her partner, was a complex figure in her own right. Despite her involvement in the gang's activities, she was not a hardened criminal from the start. Her early life was filled with dreams of a different future, and her poetry, written during the fugitive years, reveals a reflective and introspective side. One of her most famous poems, "The Story of Bonnie and Clyde," penned just weeks before their deaths, provides a poignant glimpse into her thoughts and feelings, capturing the fatalistic awareness of their impending doom.

Clyde Barrow, driven by a deep-seated resentment against the injustices he perceived, saw his life of crime as a means of striking back at a world that had offered him little opportunity. His actions were not just about survival but also a rebellion against the socio-economic conditions of the time. Yet, his methods and choices brought about only destruction and death, leading to a legacy that is both romanticized and condemned.

The enduring fascination with Bonnie and Clyde lies in the duality of their story. They were products of their time, shaped by the harsh realities of the Great Depression and the pervasive violence of the era. Their love story, played out against a backdrop of crime and pursuit, adds a layer of tragedy that resonates with audiences even today. The tension between their human vulnerabilities and their ruthless actions creates a complex narrative that continues to intrigue historians, filmmakers, and the general public.

In exploring the lives of Bonnie and Clyde, one must navigate the fine line between myth and reality. Their story is a reminder of how history can be both lived and constructed, shaped by the actions of individuals and the interpretations of those who follow. It challenges us to consider the broader social and economic contexts that produce such figures and to reflect on the ways in which their stories are told and retold through the lens of culture and memory.

Chapter 19: Frank Abagnale

Frank Abagnale, one of the most notorious con artists of the 20th century, lived a life that reads like a Hollywood script, complete with audacious frauds, remarkable escapes, and a stunning turn from fugitive to fraud prevention expert. Born on April 27, 1948, in Bronxville, New York, Frank William Abagnale Jr. was the third of four children. His father, Frank Abagnale Sr., was a successful businessman and his mother, Paulette, was of French-Algerian descent. Their seemingly stable and prosperous life took a sharp turn when his parents divorced when Frank was just 16 years old, a traumatic event that set the stage for his future criminal exploits.

Abagnale's criminal career began almost by accident. At the age of 16, he ran away from home following his parents' divorce, and with only $200 in his bank account, he quickly realized that he needed money to survive. His first con involved using his father's gasoline credit card to buy tires, batteries, and other car-related items, which he then sold at a discount to pocket the cash. This scam netted him thousands of dollars but eventually caught up with him when his father was held accountable for the charges.

Facing a dire financial situation, Abagnale turned to more sophisticated forms of fraud. He discovered that he could forge checks and manipulate bank account information to his advantage. By altering the routing numbers on checks, he could deposit them into his account and withdraw money before the bank realized the checks were fake. This technique, known as "paperhanging," became one of his primary methods of fraud.

Abagnale's most famous cons, however, involved impersonation and identity theft. He assumed various professional identities, including an airline pilot, a doctor, a lawyer, and a college professor. His most well-known ruse was posing as a Pan American World Airways pilot. Inspired by the sight of uniformed pilots and their perceived prestige, Abagnale forged a pilot's license and an employee ID badge, allowing him to "deadhead" on flights. Deadheading is a practice where pilots hitch free rides on planes to reach their next assignment. This allowed him to travel for free across the world, enjoying first-class accommodations and evading authorities. Over two years, he flew to over 26 countries, living a lavish lifestyle and accumulating a wealth of travel experiences, all without ever actually flying a plane.

Abagnale's impersonation of a doctor is equally remarkable. Using a forged Harvard University medical degree, he secured a position as a resident supervisor at a Georgia hospital. Despite having no medical training, he managed to keep his cover by delegating tasks to interns and focusing on administrative duties. His charm and confidence convinced those around him of his legitimacy, and it was only by luck that no serious medical emergencies occurred under his supervision.

Another of Abagnale's notable cons was his stint as a lawyer. He forged a Columbia University law degree and passed the Louisiana bar exam after several attempts. He then secured a job with the Louisiana State Attorney General's office. This feat was particularly audacious because it required not just the appearance of legitimacy but also the ability to convincingly navigate the legal system. His tenure was cut short when a colleague, suspicious of his inexperience, began to investigate his background.

Throughout his criminal career, Abagnale relied on his innate charm, quick thinking, and an extraordinary ability to forge documents. His exploits were not only bold but often carried out with a remarkable level of sophistication. He studied the professions he impersonated, learning their jargon and procedures to maintain his cover. This attention to detail allowed him to convincingly pass himself off as an expert in fields where he had no formal training.

Despite his successes, Abagnale's life as a fugitive was fraught with danger and close calls. He was arrested multiple times in various countries, including France, Sweden, and the United States. Each time, he managed to escape or negotiate his way out of custody. One of his most daring escapes occurred in the United States, where he managed to slip away from a plane on the tarmac, posing as an undercover prison inspector. His escapes only added to his legend and the perception of him as an elusive and cunning criminal.

Abagnale's criminal activities eventually caught up with him. In 1969, at the age of 21, he was arrested in France when an Air France flight attendant recognized him from a wanted poster. Extradited to the United States, he faced multiple charges of fraud and forgery. He was sentenced to 12 years in federal prison but served only five. His early release was facilitated by his agreement to assist the federal government in investigating fraud cases and helping to prevent future crimes.

Following his release from prison, Abagnale transformed his life. Leveraging his extensive knowledge of fraud and forgery, he became a consultant and lecturer for the FBI. For over 40 years, he has worked with the Bureau to develop strategies for combating fraud, advising on matters of document security and financial crimes. His insights have been invaluable in helping law enforcement agencies and financial institutions understand the methods of con artists and implement measures to prevent such crimes.

In addition to his work with the FBI, Abagnale founded Abagnale & Associates, a consulting firm specializing in fraud prevention and cybersecurity. Through his company, he has advised numerous corporations, government agencies, and financial institutions on how to safeguard against fraud. His expertise has made him a sought-after speaker and author on the subject of financial crimes.

Abagnale's remarkable life story was immortalized in his autobiography, "Catch Me If You Can," co-written with Stan Redding and published in 1980. The book details his criminal exploits and his transformation into a respected authority on fraud prevention. It was later adapted into a highly successful film of the same name, directed by Steven Spielberg and starring Leonardo DiCaprio as Abagnale and Tom Hanks as FBI agent Carl Hanratty, a character based on the real-life agent who pursued him. The film's success brought Abagnale's story to a global audience, cementing his place in popular culture as one of the most fascinating figures in the history of crime.

Despite the sensational nature of his past, Abagnale has consistently expressed remorse for his actions and emphasized the importance of ethical behavior and personal integrity. He has used his unique perspective to advocate for stronger security measures and to educate the public about the dangers of identity theft and financial fraud. His transformation from a notorious con artist to a respected consultant and educator is a testament to his resilience and ability to reinvent himself.

Abagnale's life is a compelling study of the complexities of human behavior and the capacity for change. His early years as a criminal were driven by a combination of desperation, ingenuity, and a desire for adventure. However, his later years have been characterized by a genuine commitment to making amends and using his knowledge for the greater good. This duality makes him a unique and multifaceted figure, whose story offers valuable lessons about the consequences of deception and the potential for redemption.

Chapter 20: Frank James

Frank James, born Alexander Franklin James on January 10, 1843, was an American outlaw who became infamous for his association with the James-Younger Gang, alongside his younger brother, Jesse James. Frank James' life and legacy are intertwined with the turbulent history of post-Civil War America, particularly in the Western frontier where lawlessness often ruled and vigilante justice was common. His story is a complex tapestry of war, family loyalty, crime, and eventual redemption.

Frank James was born in Clay County, Missouri, to Robert S. James and Zerelda Cole James. His father was a prosperous farmer and Baptist minister who moved the family to Missouri from Kentucky. Tragically, Robert James died in 1850 while on a gold prospecting trip to California, leaving Zerelda to raise their children alone. Zerelda was a strong-willed woman who would become a significant influence on Frank and his brother Jesse, instilling in them a fierce loyalty to family.

The James family's life was disrupted by the onset of the American Civil War. Missouri, a border state with divided loyalties, became a hotbed of guerrilla warfare. Frank James, influenced by the pro-Southern sentiments of his family and community, joined the Confederate cause. In 1861, at the age of 18, he enlisted in the Missouri State Guard under the command of Colonel John T. Hughes. He participated in several early skirmishes, including the Battle of Wilson's Creek, where he demonstrated courage and tactical skill.

As the war progressed, Frank joined the notorious guerrilla group led by William Clarke Quantrill, known as Quantrill's Raiders. This band of Confederate irregulars conducted brutal raids and ambushes against Union forces and pro-Union civilians, employing tactics that were often ruthless and violent. Frank James' time with Quantrill's Raiders shaped his future as an outlaw, as he became adept at guerrilla warfare, ambush tactics, and the harsh realities of survival in a lawless environment.

One of the most infamous acts committed by Quantrill's Raiders was the raid on Lawrence, Kansas, in August 1863. This attack on the pro-Union town resulted in the massacre of over 150 men and boys, and the destruction of much of the town. Frank James was part of this raid, which left an indelible mark on his reputation and foreshadowed his later involvement in violent crimes. The brutal nature of the raid, and similar actions throughout Missouri and Kansas, contributed to the deep-seated animosity between the pro-Confederate and pro-Union factions in the region.

After the Civil War ended in 1865, Frank James returned to Missouri. The post-war period was marked by chaos and economic hardship, particularly in the border states. Former Confederates, like Frank and Jesse James, found it difficult to reintegrate into society. The Reconstruction era brought with it federal occupation and the establishment of Radical Republican governments in Southern states, further fueling resentment among former Confederate sympathizers. This volatile environment set the stage for the emergence of outlaw gangs as disaffected men sought to reclaim their sense of autonomy and resist perceived injustices.

Frank and Jesse James, along with their cousins, the Younger brothers (Cole, Jim, John, and Bob), and other former guerrillas, formed what became known as the James-Younger Gang. This group of outlaws embarked on a series of daring robberies that targeted banks, trains, and stagecoaches across the Midwest. Their criminal activities began in earnest in February 1866, with the robbery of the Clay County Savings Association in Liberty, Missouri. This heist, which netted the gang a substantial sum of money, is often cited as the first daylight bank robbery in American history.

The James-Younger Gang's robberies were characterized by meticulous planning, swift execution, and a readiness to use violence.

Their familiarity with guerrilla warfare tactics, honed during the Civil War, gave them an edge over law enforcement. They employed strategies such as diversion, surprise attacks, and rapid getaways on horseback, making it difficult for authorities to apprehend them. The gang's exploits quickly captured the public's imagination, and the media of the time sensationalized their activities, often romanticizing them as Robin Hood-like figures who defied corrupt institutions.

Despite the romanticized image, the reality of the James-Younger Gang's crimes was far more brutal. Their robberies frequently resulted in bloodshed, with bank employees, law enforcement officers, and innocent bystanders killed in the crossfire. The gang's willingness to kill to achieve their aims made them feared and despised by many. One particularly notorious incident was the 1874 train robbery at Gads Hill, Missouri, where the gang robbed passengers and looted the express car, leaving a trail of terror in their wake.

As the gang's notoriety grew, so did the pressure from law enforcement and private detectives, such as the Pinkerton National Detective Agency. The Pinkertons, hired by railroad companies and banks to bring the gang to justice, employed aggressive and often ruthless tactics in their pursuit. In 1875, a botched raid by the Pinkertons on the James family farm in Kearney, Missouri, resulted in the death of Frank and Jesse's half-brother, Archie, and the maiming of their mother, Zerelda. This tragic event further entrenched the James brothers' resolve to continue their outlaw ways and heightened their vendetta against the authorities.

The turning point for the James-Younger Gang came in 1876, with the failed robbery of the First National Bank in Northfield, Minnesota. The gang, underestimating the resolve of the local townspeople, encountered fierce resistance. A gunfight ensued, resulting in the deaths of two gang members and several townspeople. The Younger brothers were captured, but Frank and Jesse managed to escape, albeit wounded and on the run. This botched robbery marked the beginning of the end for the gang.

In the years following the Northfield raid, Frank and Jesse lived as fugitives, adopting various aliases and moving frequently to avoid capture. Despite their efforts to remain hidden, they continued to commit robberies sporadically. The relentless pursuit by law enforcement, coupled with the increasing dangers and the loss of trusted comrades, began to take a toll on them. Jesse's paranoia grew, straining relationships within their shrinking circle of allies.

In 1882, Jesse James was killed by Robert Ford, a member of his own gang, who had been promised a reward by the governor of Missouri. Jesse's death marked a significant turning point for Frank. Unlike his brother, Frank had grown weary of the outlaw life and the constant threat of capture or death. The loss of his brother, combined with the relentless pressure from authorities, led Frank to consider surrendering.

On October 5, 1882, Frank James walked into the office of Missouri Governor Thomas Crittenden and surrendered himself to the authorities. His decision to turn himself in was driven by a desire to avoid the violent fate that had befallen his brother and to protect his family. Frank was tried for his crimes in Missouri and Alabama, but despite overwhelming evidence against him, he was acquitted in both cases. His acquittal can be attributed to several factors, including the lack of reliable witnesses, public sympathy for his Confederate past, and the skillful defense mounted by his attorneys.

Following his acquittal, Frank James attempted to live a law-abiding life. He worked various jobs, including as a shoe salesman and a theater doorman. In 1903, he even took part in a stage show that reenacted his life as an outlaw, capitalizing on his notoriety. Despite his efforts to go straight, Frank remained a figure of public fascination and a symbol of the violent and tumultuous era in which he lived.

Frank James spent his later years in peace, living with his wife, Annie, on their farm in Missouri. He remained a respected figure in his community, often entertaining visitors with stories of his outlaw past. He died on February 18, 1915, at the age of 72, leaving behind a complicated legacy. While some viewed him as a folk hero who defied corrupt institutions, others saw him as a ruthless criminal who left a trail of death and destruction in his wake.

The story of Frank James is a testament to the complexity of the American frontier and the enduring allure of the outlaw figure in American culture. His life, shaped by the Civil War, family loyalty, and a defiance of authority, reflects the broader social and economic upheavals of the 19th century. The romanticized image of Frank and Jesse James as Robin Hood-like figures continues to captivate the public imagination, even as historians strive to separate myth from reality.

Frank James' legacy is a reminder of the harsh realities of life on the American frontier, where violence and lawlessness were often the order of the day. His story, marked by moments of daring and brutality, courage and ruthlessness, offers a window into a world where the boundaries between hero and villain were frequently blurred. As such, Frank James remains a complex and enduring figure in the history of the American West, embodying both the romance and the harshness of that turbulent era.

Chapter 21: John "Red" Hamilton

John "Red" Hamilton, born on January 27, 1899, in Canada, was an infamous bank robber and member of the John Dillinger gang during the early 1930s. His life of crime, marked by a series of daring bank heists, prison escapes, and shootouts with law enforcement, paints a vivid picture of the tumultuous era of the Great Depression. Hamilton's story is one of desperation, loyalty, and the pursuit of wealth through illicit means, set against the backdrop of a country grappling with economic hardship and social upheaval.

Hamilton's early life remains somewhat obscure, but it is known that he was born in Canada and later moved to the United States. By the time he reached adulthood, Hamilton had already begun to establish a criminal record. His nickname "Red" came from his distinctive reddish hair, which became a recognizable feature as he gained notoriety. Hamilton's criminal career began with petty theft and small-time crimes, but he soon graduated to more serious offenses, including armed robbery.

Hamilton's entry into the world of high-profile bank robberies came when he joined forces with John Dillinger, one of the most notorious criminals of the time. Dillinger's gang, which operated primarily in the Midwest, became infamous for their bold and meticulously planned bank heists. The gang's exploits were marked by their use of military-style tactics, including the use of machine guns and bulletproof vests, which allowed them to overpower law enforcement and escape with large sums of money.

Hamilton's association with Dillinger began in the early 1930s, a period when the United States was in the grip of the Great Depression. The economic collapse had left millions unemployed and desperate, and this environment of widespread poverty and discontent provided fertile ground for outlaws who were willing to take bold risks to secure their fortunes. Dillinger and his gang, including Hamilton, capitalized on this desperation, often finding sympathizers among the public who viewed them as modern-day Robin Hoods, defying a corrupt system.

One of Hamilton's first major heists with Dillinger's gang took place on June 10, 1933, when they robbed the New Carlisle National Bank in New Carlisle, Ohio. This robbery was executed with precision and highlighted Hamilton's growing expertise in bank robbery. The gang made off with $10,600, a significant sum at the time, and managed to evade capture. This successful heist marked the beginning of a series of bank robberies that would cement Hamilton's reputation as a skilled and daring criminal.

Hamilton's role within the Dillinger gang was significant. He was not only a reliable partner in crime but also demonstrated remarkable loyalty to his comrades. This loyalty was put to the test on several occasions, particularly during the gang's numerous encounters with law enforcement. One such encounter occurred on October 12, 1933, in Mason City, Iowa, where the gang staged another successful bank robbery. However, during their escape, a violent shootout ensued with police officers, highlighting the dangerous and precarious nature of their criminal activities.

Despite the increasing pressure from law enforcement, Hamilton and the Dillinger gang continued their spree of bank robberies. On January 15, 1934, they robbed the First National Bank in East Chicago, Indiana. This heist was particularly significant because it resulted in the death of Officer William O'Malley, who was shot and killed during the robbery. The killing of a law enforcement officer escalated the gang's notoriety and intensified the manhunt for Dillinger, Hamilton, and their associates.

The gang's criminal activities eventually led to a series of arrests and imprisonments. In 1933, Hamilton was captured and incarcerated at Michigan City Prison in Indiana. However, the loyalty and resourcefulness of the Dillinger gang came to the forefront when, on September 26, 1933, Dillinger orchestrated a daring escape from the prison, freeing Hamilton and several other gang members. This escape demonstrated the gang's commitment to each other and their willingness to go to extreme lengths to secure their freedom.

Following his escape from Michigan City Prison, Hamilton resumed his criminal activities with renewed vigor. The gang's most infamous heist occurred on March 6, 1934, when they robbed the First National Bank in Sioux Falls, South Dakota. This robbery was marked by its high level of violence and meticulous planning. The gang made off with $49,500, a staggering amount of money during the Great Depression. However, the success of this heist came at a cost, as the gang's notoriety reached new heights, and the FBI intensified its efforts to apprehend them.

Hamilton's luck began to run out as the pressure from law enforcement increased. On April 23, 1934, a shootout occurred at the Little Bohemia Lodge in Manitowish Waters, Wisconsin. The Dillinger gang had been using the lodge as a hideout when they were ambushed by FBI agents. The ensuing gunfight resulted in the deaths of several individuals, including civilians, and the wounding of several gang members. Hamilton was critically injured during the shootout, suffering a gunshot wound to the back.

Despite his injuries, Hamilton managed to escape the Little Bohemia Lodge with the help of his fellow gang members. However, his condition continued to deteriorate, and the gang was forced to seek medical help for him. They turned to Dr. Joseph Moran, a former physician who had been struck off the medical register and was now working with the criminal underworld. Moran attempted to treat Hamilton's injuries, but the bullet wound became infected, and Hamilton's health declined rapidly.

John "Red" Hamilton's life came to a tragic end on April 30, 1934, just days after the Little Bohemia shootout. He succumbed to his injuries, and his body was buried in an unmarked grave near Aurora, Illinois. The exact location of his burial site remains a mystery, as the gang went to great lengths to conceal his death and avoid further scrutiny from law enforcement. Hamilton's death marked the end of his brief but notorious career as an outlaw.

The legacy of John "Red" Hamilton is intertwined with the larger narrative of the Dillinger gang and the era of the Great Depression. His life of crime, marked by daring bank heists and violent encounters with law enforcement, reflects the desperation and volatility of the time. Hamilton's story also highlights the themes of loyalty and camaraderie among the gang members, who often risked their lives to protect each other.

Hamilton's exploits, along with those of Dillinger and other gang members, captured the public's imagination and have been immortalized in popular culture. Their audacious bank robberies and dramatic shootouts with law enforcement have been depicted in numerous books, films, and television shows, cementing their place in American folklore. The romanticized image of the outlaws as antiheroes, challenging a corrupt system, continues to resonate with audiences, even as the reality of their violent and criminal actions is acknowledged.

Chapter 22: Thug Behram

Thug Behram, also known as Buhram Jamedar, stands as one of history's most notorious and enigmatic criminals. Active during the late 18th and early 19th centuries in India, Behram is infamously remembered as a leader of the Thuggee cult, a secretive organization of assassins who were feared across the Indian subcontinent. His name is often associated with an astonishing number of murders, making him one of the deadliest serial killers in recorded history. The legend of Thug Behram provides a window into a dark and complex chapter of Indian history, blending elements of mythology, colonial narratives, and the gruesome reality of organized crime.

The Thuggee cult, to which Behram belonged, was a confederation of professional assassins who traced their origins back several centuries. The Thugs, as they were known, operated under the guise of travelers, pilgrims, or merchants, blending seamlessly into the landscape of rural India. They were bound by a set of secret rituals and codes, and they worshipped the Hindu goddess Kali, whom they believed required human sacrifices. The Thugs' method of killing was both ritualistic and efficient: they used a rumaal, a ceremonial handkerchief or cloth, to strangle their victims, ensuring a swift and silent death.

Behram was born around 1765, likely in a small village in the Indian subcontinent. Little is known about his early life, but it is believed that he was introduced to the Thuggee way of life at a young age. He quickly rose through the ranks due to his cunning, ruthlessness, and unwavering loyalty to the cult's traditions. Behram's proficiency in the art of strangulation and his leadership skills eventually earned him the title of "Jamedar," a commander or chief within the Thug hierarchy.

Under Behram's leadership, the Thuggee cult reached new heights of infamy. He was reputedly involved in the murders of over 900 people, though some estimates place the number as high as 931. These killings were not random acts of violence but carefully orchestrated executions carried out during the gang's travels across the vast and often lawless stretches of rural India. Behram's victims included wealthy merchants, unsuspecting travelers, and even fellow Thugs who violated the cult's codes or posed a threat to his authority.

The Thugs' modus operandi involved infiltrating groups of travelers, gaining their trust, and then striking when their victims were most vulnerable. They often operated in well-coordinated groups, with each member playing a specific role. Scouts identified potential victims, while other members distracted and isolated the targets. The actual act of murder was usually carried out by the stranglers, who used their rumaals with deadly precision. The bodies were then buried or disposed of in remote locations to avoid detection.

Behram's reign of terror continued largely unchecked for decades, in part because the Thugs were skilled at covering their tracks and instilling fear in those who might oppose them. Their activities went largely unnoticed by the broader public and colonial authorities until the early 19th century when the British East India Company began to take notice of the increasing reports of disappearances and murders along key trade routes.

The British colonial administration, alarmed by the scale and audacity of the Thuggee activities, launched an extensive campaign to eradicate the cult. This effort was spearheaded by Captain William Sleeman, an officer in the British East India Company's army who became determined to dismantle the Thuggee network. Sleeman's campaign combined intelligence gathering, undercover operations, and the establishment of a dedicated Thuggee and Dacoity Department.

One of Sleeman's key strategies was to recruit informants from within the Thug ranks, offering them leniency in exchange for information. These informants, known as "approvers," provided invaluable insights into the inner workings of the Thuggee cult, including their rituals, codes, and hierarchy. Through the testimonies of these approvers, the British authorities were able to map out the extensive network of Thug operations and identify key leaders, including Behram.

Behram's downfall came in 1839 when he was finally captured by British forces. His arrest marked a turning point in the campaign against the Thugs, as it dealt a significant blow to the cult's leadership. During his interrogation, Behram confessed to his role in hundreds of murders, providing detailed accounts of his methods and the operations of the Thuggee network. His confessions were instrumental in further dismantling the cult and bringing many of its members to justice.

Behram was tried and sentenced to death, though some accounts suggest that he was ultimately hanged in 1840. His capture and execution symbolized the decline of the Thuggee cult, which gradually disintegrated under the relentless pressure of the British crackdown. By the mid-19th century, the Thuggee menace had been largely eradicated, and the cult faded into obscurity.

The legacy of Thug Behram and the Thuggee cult is a complex and controversial one. On the one hand, Behram's story is often cited as a chilling example of the capacity for organized crime and mass murder. His name has become synonymous with terror and ruthlessness, and his actions have been the subject of numerous books, films, and scholarly studies. On the other hand, some historians argue that the British colonial narrative of the Thugs was exaggerated and sensationalized, serving as a justification for the imposition of stricter control over Indian society.

The British portrayal of the Thugs as an existential threat to civil order helped to legitimize their efforts to impose law and order in India. This narrative emphasized the barbaric and superstitious nature of the Thugs, contrasting it with the rational and civilized values of the British colonial administration. Critics of this interpretation suggest that the British used the Thuggee campaign as a means to consolidate their power and justify their colonial rule.

Despite these debates, the story of Thug Behram remains a fascinating and unsettling chapter in the history of India and the British Empire. It underscores the complexities of colonialism, the clash of cultures, and the ways in which crime and punishment were intertwined with broader political and social dynamics. Behram's life, marked by violence and fear, serves as a stark reminder of the dark undercurrents that have shaped human history.

In contemporary popular culture, Thug Behram's legacy continues to captivate audiences. His story has inspired numerous adaptations in literature, film, and television, often emphasizing the macabre and sensational aspects of his life. These portrayals reflect a broader fascination with true crime and the psychology of criminality, as well as a continued interest in the mysteries and intrigues of the past.

Chapter 23: Moll Cutpurse

Moll Cutpurse, born Mary Frith in 1584, is a historical figure who has fascinated scholars, writers, and the public for centuries due to her unconventional lifestyle and defiance of societal norms. Known as the "Roaring Girl" and often depicted as an archetypal "female transgressor," Moll Cutpurse lived during the early 17th century in England, a period marked by strict gender roles and expectations. Her life story offers a remarkable glimpse into the world of London's criminal underworld and the vibrant, albeit risky, life of a woman who chose to live on her own terms in a society that often tried to constrain her.

Mary Frith was born into a family of modest means, the daughter of a shoemaker. Early on, she demonstrated a rebellious spirit that set her apart from her contemporaries. Rejecting the traditional roles expected of women in her time, Mary adopted the name Moll and began dressing in male attire, a choice that was not only socially unacceptable but also illegal. Her decision to cross-dress was more than a mere act of defiance; it symbolized her rejection of the restrictive norms imposed upon women and allowed her greater freedom of movement and action in a patriarchal society.

Moll's entry into the world of crime began with petty thefts and gradually escalated to more daring and lucrative endeavors. She became notorious for her skills as a pickpocket and a cutpurse, a term used for thieves who specialized in cutting purses or bags from unsuspecting victims. Her adeptness at these activities earned her the nickname "Moll Cutpurse." Unlike many of her male counterparts, who often operated under the cover of night, Moll was bold enough to ply her trade in broad daylight, targeting the bustling streets and markets of London.

Her criminal activities extended beyond simple theft. Moll was also involved in fencing stolen goods, using her connections within

London's underworld to facilitate the sale and distribution of illicit merchandise. Her network of contacts included other thieves, beggars, and criminals, which allowed her to thrive in the dangerous and often violent environment of the city's criminal underbelly. Moll's ability to navigate this world with skill and audacity set her apart as one of the most successful and feared criminals of her time.

In addition to her criminal exploits, Moll Cutpurse was also known for her public persona and flamboyant lifestyle. She was a frequent visitor to taverns, playhouses, and other public venues, where she would often engage in bawdy behavior and challenge societal norms. Moll's preference for men's clothing was not merely a practical choice for her criminal activities but also a form of self-expression and rebellion against the gender constraints of her era. Her masculine attire and bold demeanor made her a subject of fascination and scandal, drawing the attention of both the public and the authorities.

Moll's notoriety grew to such an extent that she became a subject of literature and theater during her lifetime. One of the most famous works inspired by her life is the play "The Roaring Girl," co-written by Thomas Middleton and Thomas Dekker, which premiered in 1611. The play presents a fictionalized account of Moll's exploits and character, portraying her as a witty, fearless, and independent woman who defies societal expectations. "The Roaring Girl" helped cement Moll's status as a cultural icon and contributed to the enduring legend of her life.

Despite her criminal activities, Moll Cutpurse also had moments of notoriety that blurred the lines between criminality and entertainment. She was known to perform in public, often singing and playing musical instruments, further enhancing her reputation as a multifaceted and unconventional figure. These performances, combined with her daring thefts and public appearances, made her a well-known personality in London, admired by some and reviled by others.

Moll's relationship with the law was complex. While she was frequently arrested and imprisoned for her crimes, her defiant spirit and resourcefulness often allowed her to escape severe punishment. On one notable occasion, she was arrested for cross-dressing and brought before the infamous Star Chamber, an English court known for its harsh judgments. Instead of showing remorse, Moll reportedly defended her actions with wit and confidence, impressing the court with her audacity. Her ability to navigate the legal system and maintain her freedom, despite her criminal activities, further contributed to her legend.

In 1614, Moll's life took a significant turn when she was arrested for her involvement in a robbery. This time, she faced the possibility of severe punishment, including execution. However, Moll managed to secure a pardon, likely through the influence of powerful friends and patrons who admired her spirit and found her useful for their own purposes. Following this close call, Moll appeared to retire from her life of crime, at least publicly.

In her later years, Moll Cutpurse attempted to transform her public image and sought respectability. She established herself as a bawd, running a brothel in London, and continued to be involved in the criminal underworld, albeit in a less conspicuous manner. Despite her efforts to present a more respectable front, her past and her continued involvement in illicit activities ensured that she remained a controversial figure.

Moll Cutpurse's death in 1659 marked the end of an extraordinary life that defied the conventions of her time. She was buried in the churchyard of St. Bride's Church in Fleet Street, London, leaving behind a legacy that has continued to captivate and intrigue people for centuries. Her life story, filled with bold defiance, criminal enterprise, and public performances, offers a unique perspective on the social and cultural dynamics of early modern England.

Moll's enduring legacy is reflected in the way she has been remembered and portrayed in literature, theater, and popular culture. She represents a challenge to the rigid gender norms and societal expectations of her time, embodying a spirit of independence and resistance that resonates with contemporary audiences. Her story also highlights the complexities of historical figures who straddle the line between criminality and cultural icon, illustrating how individuals can shape their own narratives and defy the constraints imposed upon them.

In the context of early modern England, Moll Cutpurse's life is particularly significant for its intersection with broader social, economic, and cultural changes. The period was marked by rapid urbanization, the expansion of trade and commerce, and shifting social dynamics, all of which created opportunities and challenges for individuals like Moll. Her ability to exploit these changes and carve out a niche for herself in a male-dominated society speaks to her resourcefulness and resilience.

Moreover, Moll's story sheds light on the criminal underworld of London, revealing the intricate networks and social structures that supported illicit activities. Her involvement in fencing stolen goods, running a brothel, and maintaining connections with other criminals illustrates the complexity of the underground economy and the ways in which it intersected with the broader society. This aspect of her life provides valuable insights into the hidden mechanisms of urban life in early modern England.

The cultural impact of Moll Cutpurse is also evident in the way she has been mythologized and reinterpreted over time. Her depiction in "The Roaring Girl" and other literary works reflects the fascination with transgressive female figures who challenge societal norms and embody a sense of rebellious freedom. This fascination continues in contemporary interpretations, where Moll is often celebrated as a proto-feminist icon, a woman who asserted her autonomy and refused to be constrained by the expectations of her gender.

Chapter 24: Stede Bonnet

Stede Bonnet, often referred to as the "Gentleman Pirate," is one of the most intriguing figures in the annals of piracy. His life and career offer a fascinating study of a man who defied his genteel origins to embark on a short but eventful life of crime on the high seas. Born around 1688 in Bridgetown, Barbados, to a wealthy English family, Bonnet's story is a stark departure from the typical narrative of pirates, who were often driven to their criminal enterprises by poverty or desperation. Instead, Bonnet's foray into piracy seems almost inexplicable given his privileged background, making his tale one of the most peculiar in maritime history.

Bonnet inherited a substantial estate upon the death of his parents, which provided him with financial stability and a position of respect within Barbadian society. He married Mary Allamby, and the couple had three sons and a daughter. Despite his comfortable lifestyle, Bonnet grew increasingly dissatisfied with his life. The reasons for his discontent are not entirely clear, but contemporary accounts suggest he was experiencing marital strife and a midlife crisis, which may have contributed to his decision to turn to piracy.

In 1717, at the age of around 29, Bonnet made the extraordinary decision to abandon his comfortable life and take to the sea as a pirate. He commissioned the construction of a sloop, which he named the "Revenge," and funded its outfitting entirely from his own wealth. This act alone set him apart from other pirates, who typically captured their vessels or came into piracy through more desperate means. Bonnet hired a crew of over seventy men, offering them wages rather than shares of plunder, which was another unusual practice in the pirate community. This method of recruitment reflected his lack of experience and understanding of pirate traditions.

Bonnet's early exploits as a pirate were marked by a combination of naivety and ambition. He initially sailed along the American East

Coast and the Caribbean, targeting merchant vessels. His lack of naval experience became evident in these early ventures, as he often relied heavily on his crew for navigation and combat tactics. Despite his shortcomings, Bonnet managed to capture a number of ships, including the "Anne" and the "Turbet."

Bonnet's activities soon drew the attention of more experienced pirates, including the infamous Edward Teach, better known as Blackbeard. In August 1717, Bonnet encountered Blackbeard off the coast of North Carolina. Recognizing Bonnet's lack of experience, Blackbeard took advantage of the situation. He suggested an alliance and persuaded Bonnet to allow him to take temporary command of the "Revenge." Bonnet, who was recovering from a severe injury sustained in a recent battle, reluctantly agreed. Under Blackbeard's command, the "Revenge" joined Blackbeard's flotilla, which included the flagship "Queen Anne's Revenge."

For several months, Bonnet sailed under Blackbeard's shadow, learning the ropes of piracy. Blackbeard's influence was significant, and during this period, Bonnet's piratical prowess improved. However, Bonnet's relationship with Blackbeard was strained, characterized by mutual mistrust and exploitation. Blackbeard eventually betrayed Bonnet, seizing control of the "Revenge" and abandoning Bonnet and his men on a small island near the Bay of Honduras.

Bonnet and his crew were rescued by another pirate, Charles Vane, and they soon regained control of the "Revenge." Determined to reassert himself as a pirate captain, Bonnet adopted the alias "Captain Thomas" and resumed his piratical activities. His next series of raids along the Eastern Seaboard of America were more successful, though his reputation never fully recovered from his association with Blackbeard.

In the summer of 1718, Bonnet attempted to take advantage of a royal pardon offered to pirates by the colonial authorities. He sailed to Bath Town in North Carolina and surrendered to Governor Charles

Eden, hoping to receive a pardon and start anew as a privateer. Despite receiving the pardon, Bonnet could not resist the lure of piracy. He resumed his criminal activities shortly after, violating the terms of his pardon and once again becoming a wanted man.

Bonnet's final chapter began in August 1718 when he sailed to Cape Fear River to make repairs to the "Revenge." While there, he encountered Colonel William Rhett, a pirate hunter from South Carolina. Rhett engaged Bonnet in a fierce battle known as the Battle of Cape Fear River. After a protracted and bloody confrontation, Bonnet and his crew were captured. They were taken to Charleston, South Carolina, where they were imprisoned and awaited trial.

Bonnet's trial was a significant event, attracting widespread attention due to his status as the "Gentleman Pirate." The trial proceedings revealed much about his piratical activities and his motivations. Despite his attempts to mount a defense and argue that he had been forced into piracy, Bonnet was found guilty of multiple counts of piracy. On November 10, 1718, he was sentenced to death.

In the weeks following his trial, Bonnet made a desperate attempt to escape from prison, but he was quickly recaptured. His execution was carried out on December 10, 1718. Bonnet was hanged at White Point Garden in Charleston, bringing an end to his brief and tumultuous career as a pirate.

Stede Bonnet's legacy is a complex one. His life as a pirate was marked by a series of contradictions and missteps, yet he remains a fascinating figure due to his unique background and the audacity of his decision to embrace a life of crime. Unlike many of his contemporaries, Bonnet's foray into piracy was not driven by economic necessity or social marginalization but rather by a personal crisis and a desire for adventure. This makes his story an anomaly in the history of piracy.

Bonnet's exploits have been romanticized and fictionalized in various works of literature and popular culture. His story has been the subject of novels, plays, and television series, all of which explore the intriguing paradox of a wealthy landowner turning to piracy. His association with Blackbeard adds another layer of interest, as it places him in the context of some of the most notorious figures of the Golden Age of Piracy.

Historians continue to debate the motivations behind Bonnet's actions. Some suggest that his midlife crisis and dissatisfaction with his domestic life pushed him towards a drastic change. Others argue that Bonnet may have been seeking to emulate the romanticized image of pirates as free and adventurous spirits, rebelling against societal norms and constraints. Whatever the reasons, Bonnet's story remains a testament to the unpredictability of human behavior and the lengths to which individuals will go in pursuit of their desires.

In examining Bonnet's life, it is also important to consider the broader context of piracy during the early 18th century. The Golden Age of Piracy was a time of significant upheaval and transformation in the Atlantic world. The decline of European colonial powers, coupled with the expansion of maritime trade, created opportunities for piracy to flourish. Pirates like Bonnet and Blackbeard exploited these opportunities, challenging the authority of colonial governments and disrupting commercial shipping routes.

Bonnet's story also sheds light on the complexities of pirate society. Pirates operated under a unique set of codes and practices that distinguished them from other criminals. They often established their own systems of governance and shared their plunder according to agreed-upon rules. Despite his initial lack of understanding of these practices, Bonnet eventually adapted to the pirate way of life, demonstrating the adaptability and resilience that characterized many successful pirates.

Chapter 25: Blackbeard (Edward Teach)

Edward Teach, better known as Blackbeard, remains one of the most infamous and feared pirates in maritime history. His moniker evokes a sense of dread and adventure, symbolizing the golden age of piracy in the early 18th century. Blackbeard's life, filled with daring exploits, brutal confrontations, and a notorious reputation, has been the subject of countless tales, legends, and historical accounts. His story, while often shrouded in myth, offers a fascinating glimpse into the world of piracy and the turbulent seas of the Caribbean and the Atlantic.

Blackbeard was likely born around 1680, though his early life remains largely undocumented. Most historians agree he was born in Bristol, England, a significant port city known for its maritime activities. His given name was Edward Teach, though various sources also record it as Thatch or Thach. Teach's formative years likely involved a career in sailing or privateering, a legally sanctioned form of piracy that allowed private ships to attack enemy vessels during wartime. This background would have provided Teach with valuable nautical skills and combat experience, setting the stage for his later career as a pirate.

By the early 1710s, Teach had moved to the Caribbean, a region teeming with piracy. It was here that he first joined the crew of Benjamin Hornigold, a notorious pirate captain. Hornigold, recognizing Teach's abilities, quickly promoted him to command a captured sloop. Teach's rise through the pirate ranks was swift, and he soon began to establish his fearsome reputation. His physical appearance contributed significantly to his notoriety; Teach was a tall, imposing figure with a thick black beard that he braided and tied with ribbons. To enhance his terrifying image, he would place slow-burning fuses in his beard and hat during battles, creating a fearsome spectacle of smoke and fire that struck terror into the hearts of his enemies.

Teach's most significant exploit began in late 1717 when he captured a large French slave ship named "La Concorde." He renamed the vessel "Queen Anne's Revenge" and outfitted it with 40 guns, making it one of the most formidable ships in the pirate fleet. Under the flag of Queen Anne's Revenge, Blackbeard embarked on a series of high-profile raids, targeting merchant ships along the American coast and the Caribbean. His exploits were marked by both cunning strategy and brutal force, earning him a reputation as one of the most feared pirates of his time.

One of Blackbeard's most audacious acts occurred in May 1718, when he blockaded the port of Charleston, South Carolina. For nearly a week, he captured incoming and outgoing ships, demanding a ransom from the city. His primary demand was for a chest of medicine, which he eventually received, demonstrating his ability to hold entire towns hostage to his whims. This incident further solidified his fearsome reputation and demonstrated his strategic prowess in exploiting the weaknesses of colonial authorities.

Following the blockade of Charleston, Blackbeard sailed north to North Carolina. There, he sought and received a pardon from Governor Charles Eden under the Act of Grace, a royal decree offering clemency to pirates who surrendered within a specified period. Blackbeard briefly retired to a life of relative obscurity, but it wasn't long before he returned to his piratical ways. He established a base of operations on Ocracoke Island, using its remote location as a haven for his fleet and a staging ground for further raids.

Blackbeard's activities soon drew the ire of the colonial authorities, particularly Governor Alexander Spotswood of Virginia. Determined to rid the seas of the pirate menace, Spotswood launched a concerted effort to capture Blackbeard. He enlisted the help of Lieutenant Robert Maynard of the Royal Navy, who set sail with two sloops to confront the pirate. On November 22, 1718, Maynard's forces engaged Blackbeard and his crew off the coast of Ocracoke Island in a fierce battle.

The confrontation between Maynard and Blackbeard has become the stuff of legend. Blackbeard's crew initially had the upper hand, but Maynard employed a cunning ruse. He ordered most of his men to hide below deck, giving the appearance that his ship had been severely damaged and was nearly deserted. When Blackbeard and his men boarded Maynard's vessel, they were met with a surprise counterattack. The battle that ensued was brutal and bloody, with hand-to-hand combat taking place on the decks of the ships. Blackbeard, despite his formidable presence and fighting prowess, was eventually overwhelmed. He was reportedly shot five times and received more than twenty sword wounds before finally succumbing to his injuries.

Maynard beheaded Blackbeard and displayed his severed head on the bowsprit of his ship as a grim trophy and a warning to other pirates. Blackbeard's death marked the end of an era in the history of piracy. His capture and execution were celebrated by colonial authorities and heralded as a significant victory in the ongoing struggle to suppress piracy in the Atlantic and the Caribbean.

The legacy of Blackbeard, however, extends far beyond his death. His fearsome image and legendary exploits have cemented his place in popular culture as the quintessential pirate. Stories of his buried treasure, his fearsome appearance, and his ruthless tactics have been immortalized in books, films, and folklore. Blackbeard's character has become a staple in pirate-themed media, embodying the romanticized image of the swashbuckling pirate.

Historical accounts of Blackbeard vary, with some contemporary sources portraying him as a brutal and ruthless villain, while others suggest he was a more complex figure, employing fear and intimidation as tools of psychological warfare rather than sheer brutality. Some historians argue that Blackbeard's reputation for cruelty was exaggerated by his enemies and the colonial authorities who sought to vilify him as a means of justifying their efforts to eradicate piracy.

In addition to his fearsome persona, Blackbeard was known for his leadership and tactical acumen. He commanded a loyal crew and managed a diverse fleet of ships, coordinating raids and blockades with precision. His ability to navigate the treacherous waters of the Caribbean and the Atlantic, as well as his strategic use of coastal hideouts, demonstrated a keen understanding of maritime warfare.

Blackbeard's impact on the history of piracy is significant not only for his personal exploits but also for the broader implications of his actions. His activities highlighted the vulnerabilities of colonial shipping and trade routes, prompting increased efforts to protect commerce and suppress piracy. The measures taken by colonial governments, including the use of naval forces and the offer of pardons to pirates, reflected a growing recognition of the need for coordinated responses to the threat posed by pirates like Blackbeard.

The mythos surrounding Blackbeard has also contributed to the enduring fascination with piracy as a cultural phenomenon. The image of the pirate, with its associations of adventure, rebellion, and freedom, continues to captivate the popular imagination. Blackbeard, as one of the most iconic figures of the Golden Age of Piracy, represents the allure and danger of the pirate life, embodying the tension between the romanticized ideal and the harsh realities of piracy.

Chapter 26: Claude Duval

Claude Duval, an infamous highwayman of the 17th century, remains one of the most romanticized figures in the history of crime. His life story, shrouded in both historical facts and legendary embellishments, paints a picture of a charming and chivalrous rogue who captured the public's imagination. Born in 1643 in Domfront, Normandy, France, Duval's transition from humble beginnings to becoming a notorious highwayman in England is a tale marked by adventure, romance, and a dramatic end.

Duval was born into a relatively modest family. His father was a miller, which likely provided the family with a stable, albeit humble, livelihood. The political turmoil of the English Civil War, which also impacted France, created an environment ripe for a young man seeking adventure. As a youth, Duval was reportedly sent to Paris, where he found employment with an English family. This exposure to English culture and language would prove crucial in his later life.

The Restoration of Charles II to the English throne in 1660 marked a period of significant change in England. Duval, like many others, was drawn to the opportunities presented by the newly restored monarchy and the bustling city of London. He arrived in England as part of the entourage of the English aristocracy returning from exile in France. Duval's charming demeanor and good looks quickly earned him a reputation among the elite circles of London society.

However, Duval's entry into the world of crime seems to have been driven by a combination of necessity and opportunity. The Restoration period, while prosperous for some, also saw many soldiers and retainers of the former Commonwealth army left without employment. The highways of England, particularly those leading to and from London, became increasingly dangerous as bands of highwaymen preyed on wealthy travelers. Duval found this environment conducive to his particular set of skills.

Duval's modus operandi was distinct from that of other highwaymen of his time. He cultivated an image of the gentleman-robber, a courteous and gallant figure who eschewed unnecessary violence. Stories of his exploits often highlight his charm and wit. One of the most famous anecdotes about Duval involves his robbery of a coach carrying a nobleman and his wife. According to the legend, instead of immediately demanding their valuables, Duval courteously invited the lady to dance with him by the roadside. After the dance, he politely requested the nobleman to hand over his money, a request that was reportedly granted without protest. This tale, whether true or apocryphal, encapsulates the romantic image of Duval that has persisted through the centuries.

Duval's career as a highwayman was marked by a series of daring and audacious robberies. He was known for his meticulous planning and the careful selection of his targets, often focusing on the wealthiest and most influential travelers. His charm and good looks endeared him to many, including some of his victims, who were often left more amused than outraged by their encounters with him. This notoriety and the stories of his gallant behavior earned him a certain level of notoriety and even a degree of grudging respect among the public.

Despite his attempts to maintain a gentlemanly facade, Duval was still a criminal, and his activities eventually drew the attention of the authorities. The increasing number of highway robberies around London led to a concerted effort to apprehend the culprits. Duval's luck ran out in 1670 when he was finally captured at the Hole-in-the-Wall tavern in London's Chandos Street. His arrest marked the beginning of the end for the dashing highwayman.

Duval's trial was a significant event, attracting considerable public interest. Despite his notoriety and the charm he had exhibited during his criminal career, the court showed little leniency. He was found guilty of highway robbery and sentenced to death. Duval's execution took place on January 21, 1670, at Tyburn, the notorious gallows in

London. His death was witnessed by a large crowd, many of whom were drawn by the tales of his exploits and his charismatic persona.

The legend of Claude Duval did not end with his death. His story was immortalized in various literary works, ballads, and later, plays and films. The romanticized image of Duval as a gallant and chivalrous rogue continued to capture the public imagination, contributing to the enduring fascination with his character. Authors and playwrights embellished his story, often portraying him as a noble figure fighting against social injustices or as a tragic hero undone by love and fate.

The historical reality of Duval's life, while certainly marked by criminal activities, was overshadowed by the myth that grew around him. This mythologizing of Duval highlights the cultural fascination with outlaws who defy societal norms and the romantic allure of the gentleman-robber archetype. His story serves as a reminder of the blurred lines between history and legend, where the truth often becomes secondary to the narrative constructed by popular culture.

The appeal of Claude Duval's story lies in its combination of adventure, romance, and rebellion. His transformation from a humble miller's son to a notorious highwayman reflects the broader social dynamics of 17th-century England, a time of significant upheaval and change. The Restoration period, with its mix of political instability and economic opportunity, provided the perfect backdrop for the rise of figures like Duval, who navigated the turbulent landscape with charm and audacity.

Duval's legacy also underscores the role of storytelling in shaping historical memory. The tales of his exploits, whether factual or fictional, have endured for centuries, illustrating the power of narrative in immortalizing individuals who capture the public's imagination. The romanticized version of Duval's life has influenced subsequent depictions of highwaymen and outlaws in literature and media, cementing his place in the cultural lexicon as the quintessential gentleman-robber.

Chapter 27: The Dalton Gang

The Dalton Gang is one of the most notorious and fascinating groups in the annals of American outlaw history, embodying the wild, lawless spirit of the Old West in the late 19th century. The gang was primarily composed of the Dalton brothers—Gratton "Grat", Bob, Emmett, and sometimes Bill Dalton—along with a rotating cast of other desperadoes. Their criminal activities spanned a brief but intensely violent period, during which they committed a series of audacious train and bank robberies, cementing their reputation as some of the most daring criminals of their time. The gang's story is marked by a transition from law enforcement to lawbreaking, a narrative arc that reflects the turbulent and often morally ambiguous nature of life on the American frontier.

The Dalton brothers were born into a family that was no stranger to hardship. Their parents, Lewis and Adeline Dalton, moved westward from Kentucky to Missouri and then to Indian Territory, in search of a better life. The family faced numerous challenges, including the death of several children and financial instability. Despite these struggles, the Daltons were known to be a tight-knit family, bound by strong familial loyalty—a trait that would later manifest in their criminal endeavors. The brothers initially sought to make an honest living. Gratton, known as "Grat", and Bob both worked as lawmen, serving as deputies in Indian Territory. Emmett, the youngest of the three, also briefly worked in law enforcement. Their time as lawmen provided them with valuable skills and knowledge that would later aid their transition to a life of crime. They learned how to handle firearms, track criminals, and navigate the rugged terrain of the West.

The Daltons' shift from lawmen to outlaws was not an abrupt transformation but rather a gradual descent into criminality, spurred by frustration with the law's limitations and a desire for quick wealth. The first significant step in their journey to infamy occurred in February

1891, when they attempted to rob a Southern Pacific Railroad train near Alila, California. This initial foray into train robbery was a bold move that demonstrated their willingness to take on significant risks for potentially high rewards. Although the heist was poorly executed and ultimately unsuccessful, it marked the beginning of their criminal career and set the tone for future exploits. Their attempt was met with strong resistance, resulting in a fierce gunfight that left one guard dead and one of the gang members, Bob Dalton, seriously wounded.

Undeterred by their initial failure, the Dalton Gang continued to target trains and banks, capitalizing on the rapid expansion of the railroad system and the establishment of new financial institutions across the frontier. They became particularly adept at train robberies, which were considered high-risk but potentially high-reward endeavors. The railroads, representing the burgeoning industrial power of the United States, were seen as lucrative targets. The Daltons meticulously planned their heists, leveraging their knowledge of railroad schedules and security measures to execute their robberies with precision and speed. They often struck in remote areas where law enforcement presence was minimal, allowing them to escape with relative ease.

One of their most infamous train robberies occurred on July 14, 1892, when the Dalton Gang targeted a train near Adair, Oklahoma. This heist was notable not only for the substantial sum of money they managed to steal but also for the violence that accompanied it. The gang's attack on the train resulted in the death of one guard and the serious wounding of several others, further cementing their reputation as ruthless and dangerous criminals. This robbery, like many others, was characterized by the gang's willingness to use deadly force to achieve their objectives. The Adair heist was a significant success for the gang, bolstering their notoriety and increasing the pressure on law enforcement to capture them.

Despite their successes, the Dalton Gang's criminal career was fraught with danger and close calls. Law enforcement agencies across multiple states were determined to bring them to justice, and the gang was constantly on the run, moving from one hideout to another to evade capture. The Daltons' ability to evade the law for as long as they did is a testament to their cunning and resourcefulness. They frequently changed their appearance, used aliases, and relied on a network of informants and sympathizers to stay one step ahead of the authorities. However, their luck would eventually run out, leading to one of the most dramatic and violent confrontations in the history of the Old West.

The gang's most audacious and ultimately disastrous endeavor was their attempt to rob two banks simultaneously in Coffeyville, Kansas, on October 5, 1892. This bold plan, if successful, would have been a historic feat and solidified their legacy as the most daring outlaws of their time. The Daltons, disguising themselves with false beards and mustaches to avoid recognition, divided their forces to simultaneously rob the First National Bank and the Condon Bank. However, their disguises did little to conceal their identities, as the townspeople quickly recognized the Daltons and raised the alarm. Coffeyville was a town on high alert, well aware of the gang's reputation and determined to defend itself against their threat. As the Daltons attempted their heist, the citizens armed themselves and prepared for a confrontation.

What followed was a fierce and bloody gun battle that left a lasting mark on the history of Coffeyville. The townspeople, including store owners, clerks, and other ordinary citizens, took up arms and confronted the gang members as they emerged from the banks. The ensuing firefight was chaotic and deadly, with bullets flying in all directions. The Daltons, outnumbered and outgunned, found themselves trapped in a deadly crossfire. The confrontation resulted in the deaths of four members of the Dalton Gang: Gratton, Bob, Dick Broadwell, and Bill Powers. Emmett Dalton, despite being severely wounded with 23 gunshot wounds, miraculously survived. The Coffeyville raid was a catastrophic failure for the gang, ending their reign of terror and marking the end of their criminal careers.

Emmett Dalton's survival and subsequent capture provided a dramatic epilogue to the gang's story. After receiving medical treatment for his injuries, Emmett was tried and sentenced to life in prison. His survival and imprisonment became a subject of widespread public interest, adding a human dimension to the otherwise grim tale of the Dalton Gang. Emmett's story of survival and redemption offered a glimpse into the complexities of the human spirit and the possibility of change, even for those who had walked a path of crime. After serving 14 years in prison, Emmett was paroled and went on to live a relatively quiet life, eventually writing a memoir that detailed the gang's exploits and his own journey from lawman to outlaw and back to a semblance of normalcy. His memoir, while providing an insider's perspective on the gang's activities, also served as a cautionary tale about the perils of a life of crime.

The legacy of the Dalton Gang is a complex and multifaceted one. On one hand, they are remembered as ruthless criminals who brought terror to the American frontier with their violent and audacious robberies. On the other hand, their story is a reflection of the broader social and economic upheavals of the time, highlighting the thin line between law and lawlessness in the rapidly changing landscape of the Old West. The Dalton brothers' transition from law enforcement to criminality underscores the moral ambiguity that often-characterized life on the frontier, where the pursuit of wealth and justice could lead individuals down perilous and unpredictable paths. Their story is not just a tale of crime and punishment but also a window into the challenges and contradictions of a rapidly expanding nation grappling with its own identity and destiny.

The Dalton Gang's exploits have been immortalized in countless books, films, and popular stories, ensuring that their legend endures in the collective memory of the American West. Their daring heists, dramatic downfall, and the personal stories of its members continue to captivate audiences, serving as a reminder of a time when the American frontier was a land of opportunity and danger, where the line between hero and villain was often indistinct. The Dalton Gang's story offers a rich and compelling narrative that encapsulates the spirit of the Old West, reflecting both the promise and the peril of a frontier society in the throes of transformation. Their legacy is a testament to the enduring fascination with the outlaws and lawmen who shaped the myth and reality of the American West, leaving an indelible mark on the nation's history and imagination.

Chapter 28: Jeanne de Clisson

Jeanne de Clisson, also known as the Lioness of Brittany, is a legendary figure whose story combines the elements of tragedy, vengeance, and defiance. Her life, marked by personal loss and a quest for retribution, took a dramatic turn that saw her becoming one of the most infamous female pirates of the 14th century. Jeanne's tale is deeply entwined with the complex political and military conflicts of her time, particularly the War of the Breton Succession, which pitted France against England in a struggle for control over the Duchy of Brittany. Her transformation from a noblewoman to a feared privateer is a compelling narrative that highlights the turbulent dynamics of medieval Europe and the extraordinary lengths to which she went to avenge her family's honor.

Jeanne de Clisson was born in 1300 into the noble de Belleville family in the Vendée region of France. Her early life was typical of a woman of her status, characterized by her upbringing in a feudal society where alliances and marriages were often politically motivated. In 1312, at the age of 12, she married her first husband, Geoffrey de Châteaubriant VIII, a nobleman who came from a powerful family. This marriage produced two children and strengthened Jeanne's position within the Breton nobility. However, tragedy struck when Geoffrey died in 1326, leaving Jeanne a widow at the age of 26.

Jeanne's second marriage was to Olivier IV de Clisson, a prominent Breton nobleman with whom she had five children. The Clisson family was deeply involved in the political affairs of Brittany, and Olivier was a key figure in the ongoing conflict between the French and English crowns. The War of the Breton Succession, which broke out in 1341 following the death of Duke John III of Brittany, created a power vacuum that led to a protracted and brutal struggle for control over the duchy. This conflict, part of the larger Hundred Years' War between England and France, saw rival factions vying for supremacy, with

Olivier de Clisson aligning himself with the French side, supporting Charles de Blois' claim to the duchy.

Olivier de Clisson's fortunes took a dire turn in 1343 when he was accused of treason by King Philip VI of France. The exact nature of the accusations remains unclear, but it is believed that Olivier may have been suspected of colluding with the English, who were vying for influence in Brittany through their support of John of Montfort, Charles de Blois' rival. Olivier was arrested and taken to Paris, where he was subjected to a swift and highly controversial trial. The trial was widely perceived as a miscarriage of justice, characterized by dubious charges and a lack of substantial evidence. Despite his protests of innocence and the appeals of his wife, Olivier was found guilty and sentenced to death.

On August 2, 1343, Olivier de Clisson was executed by beheading at the Place de l'Île-de-France in Paris. His head was subsequently displayed on a pike at the gates of Nantes as a grim warning to others who might consider betraying the French crown. This brutal and humiliating act deeply affected Jeanne de Clisson, plunging her into a state of profound grief and outrage. She viewed her husband's execution as not only an injustice but also a personal affront that demanded retribution. Fueled by a desire for vengeance, Jeanne resolved to take matters into her own hands and exact a terrible price from those she held responsible for Olivier's death.

Jeanne de Clisson's quest for revenge began with a calculated and brutal series of actions aimed at those she deemed complicit in her husband's execution. She sold off her family's lands and properties to fund her campaign of retribution, using the proceeds to raise a small army of loyal followers. Jeanne's first targets were the French nobility in Brittany who had supported King Philip VI's decision to execute Olivier. She led her forces in a series of raids against these nobles, attacking their estates, seizing their wealth, and often putting their inhabitants to the sword. These raids were characterized by their ferocity and single-minded focus on vengeance, with Jeanne sparing no effort to terrorize those who had wronged her.

Jeanne's campaign of land-based retribution eventually expanded to the sea, where she would achieve lasting notoriety as a pirate. In 1343, she equipped three warships with the funds she had amassed and set sail with a crew of loyalists, determined to wage a maritime war against the French. Jeanne's flagship was a formidable vessel known as the "My Revenge," a name that clearly signified her intentions. The ships were painted black and flew crimson sails, an intimidating sight that struck fear into the hearts of those who encountered them.

Jeanne de Clisson's piratical activities were focused primarily on the waters of the English Channel, a crucial maritime route for commerce and military supplies. Her fleet targeted French merchant ships and naval vessels, attacking them with ruthless efficiency. Jeanne's strategy involved intercepting ships bound for France, boarding them, and executing any French nobles or soldiers found on board. The crew members who were spared were often set adrift or allowed to return to port with grim tales of the Lioness of Brittany's wrath. Jeanne's actions had a significant impact on French maritime activities, disrupting trade and military logistics and causing considerable consternation among the French authorities.

Despite her fearsome reputation as a pirate, Jeanne de Clisson also maintained a degree of political acumen. She forged an alliance with the English, who were only too happy to support her efforts against their French enemies. The English crown provided her with a safe haven in their ports and, in return, Jeanne's activities contributed to the English war effort by weakening French naval power and disrupting their supply lines. This alliance with the English not only gave Jeanne's campaign legitimacy but also ensured that she had the resources and support needed to continue her vendetta against the French crown.

Jeanne's piratical activities continued for several years, during which she amassed a considerable fortune and a fearsome reputation.

Her campaign of vengeance became legendary, and her name was synonymous with terror along the French coast. Despite numerous attempts by the French navy to capture or destroy her fleet, Jeanne remained elusive, using her intimate knowledge of the waters and her superior seamanship to evade her pursuers. Her ability to operate with impunity in the English Channel is a testament to her skill as a maritime commander and her determination to avenge her husband's death.

The exact details of Jeanne de Clisson's later life is somewhat murky, but it is believed that she eventually retired from piracy around 1356. She returned to land, settling in England where she married an English nobleman, Sir Walter Bentley, a knight who had served under King Edward III during the Hundred Years' War. Jeanne's marriage to Bentley marked a new chapter in her life, one in which she left behind her life of violence and retribution. The couple eventually returned to Brittany, where they lived out their remaining years in relative peace.

Jeanne de Clisson died in 1359, leaving behind a legacy that continues to captivate and inspire. Her story is one of remarkable resilience and defiance, a tale of a woman who refused to be a victim and instead took control of her fate with extraordinary determination and courage. Jeanne's transformation from a noblewoman to a feared pirate is a testament to the complexities of medieval society and the ways in which individuals could transcend their prescribed roles to leave a lasting mark on history.

The legend of Jeanne de Clisson has endured through the centuries, inspiring numerous books, films, and other works of art. Her story has been interpreted in various ways, with some viewing her as a tragic heroine who fought against injustice, while others see her as a ruthless avenger whose actions were driven by a desire for personal retribution. Regardless of the perspective, Jeanne's life and actions continue to resonate as a powerful example of the lengths to which a person can go in the name of love and vengeance.

In contemporary discussions of Jeanne de Clisson, she is often celebrated as a symbol of female empowerment and resilience. Her ability to command a fleet and wage a successful campaign of piracy in a male-dominated world challenges traditional notions of gender roles and highlights the capacity for women to exert agency and influence in even the most challenging circumstances. Jeanne's story also serves as a reminder of the broader historical context in which she lived, a time of political upheaval and conflict that shaped the destinies of individuals and nations alike.

The tale of Jeanne de Clisson, the Lioness of Brittany, remains a compelling and enduring part of history, a narrative that combines elements of tragedy, revenge, and defiance to create a story that is both inspiring and cautionary. Her legacy as a fierce and determined avenger who challenged the power structures of her time continues to captivate the imagination and serves as a powerful reminder of the complexities of human motivation and the enduring impact of personal loss and retribution.

Chapter 29: Sawney Bean

Sawney Bean, often regarded as a mythical figure, is said to have led a notorious clan in 16th-century Scotland. This group, numbering around 48 members, is infamous in folklore for their gruesome acts of murder and cannibalism. The story of Sawney Bean is one of the most chilling and enduring legends in British folklore, encapsulating the fear of the unknown and the horrifying possibilities of human depravity. Although the veracity of the tale is debated, with many suggesting it might be more myth than fact, the narrative remains a powerful and grisly part of cultural history.

According to legend, Alexander "Sawney" Bean was born in East Lothian, Scotland, in the late 15th century. He reportedly grew up in a rural area, where he worked as a laborer, doing menial jobs. However, dissatisfied with the hard work and meager earnings, Bean decided to abandon the life of an honest laborer. He left his home with a woman named Black Agnes Douglas, who was described as equally wicked and depraved. Together, they established their lair in a coastal cave near Bennane Head in Ayrshire, a remote and rugged area that provided the perfect hideout for their nefarious activities. The cave was said to extend for several miles, allowing the Beans to evade capture and live in secrecy.

The couple began their life of crime by ambushing travelers on the secluded roads near their cave. They would rob and murder their victims, then drag the bodies back to their hideout, where they would butcher them and consume their flesh. The Beans' cannibalistic practices were not merely a matter of necessity but were also a deliberate act of terror and control. The couple's gruesome activities eventually expanded into a full-fledged clan as they produced numerous offspring, who in turn engaged in incestuous relationships, resulting in a large, inbred family. This extended clan is said to have numbered around 48 members by the time they were apprehended, comprising sons, daughters, grandsons, and granddaughters, all of whom participated in the family's gruesome acts.

The legend states that for over 25 years, the Bean clan carried out their horrific deeds, preying on travelers and locals alike. They would meticulously ambush their victims, killing them and then dismembering their bodies. The remains were reportedly salted and preserved for later consumption, a gruesome testament to the clan's systematic approach to their macabre lifestyle. The Beans' cave, located in a remote and inaccessible part of the coast, became a grisly repository of human remains, with the bones and body parts of their victims strewn about, adding to the horror of their tale. The clan's ability to evade capture for so long can be attributed to the isolated location of their hideout, the savagery of their attacks, and the general fear they instilled in the local population.

Over the years, the disappearances of travelers and locals created an atmosphere of fear and suspicion in the surrounding areas. Local authorities were baffled by the mysterious vanishings, and numerous innocent people were wrongfully accused and executed for the crimes committed by the Beans. The situation grew so dire that entire villages became too terrified to venture far from their homes, and rumors of a monstrous clan of cannibals spread like wildfire. Despite numerous searches, the Beans' cave remained undiscovered for many years, shrouded in darkness and secrecy.

The downfall of the Sawney Bean clan reportedly came about due to a fortunate escape by one of their intended victims. According to the legend, one night, the Beans ambushed a couple returning from a fair on horseback. They killed the woman but before they could dispatch her husband, a group of returning fairgoers happened upon the scene. The Bean clan, fearing capture, retreated to their cave, leaving the husband alive. He quickly reported the attack to the local authorities, who in turn notified King James VI of Scotland. Shocked by the tale of cannibalism and murder, the king led a search party of

400 men, accompanied by bloodhounds, to track down the Bean clan. After an extensive search, the party discovered the Beans' cave, the entrance to which was concealed by the tides and almost invisible to the casual observer.

Upon entering the cave, the search party was confronted with a horrifying sight: the remains of countless human bodies, dismembered and preserved for consumption. The stench of decaying flesh and the sheer scale of the carnage confirmed the unbelievable extent of the Beans' crimes. The clan was captured without resistance, their long reign of terror finally brought to an end. The Bean family, including women and children, were taken to Edinburgh, where they faced a swift and brutal form of justice. The men of the clan were executed by having their limbs cut off and left to bleed to death, a punishment deemed fitting for their heinous crimes. The women and children were burned alive, an equally horrific end for a family that had committed such unspeakable acts.

The story of Sawney Bean and his clan has been passed down through the centuries, evolving with each retelling. Some historians and scholars argue that the tale is more myth than fact, suggesting that it may have been a piece of anti-Scottish propaganda, designed to portray the Scots as barbaric and uncivilized during a time of political tension between England and Scotland. The absence of contemporary records and the fantastical elements of the story, such as the extraordinary length of time the Beans remained undetected and the sheer number of victims, support the theory that the Sawney Bean story is a blend of folklore and fear rather than a historical account.

Despite its likely fictional origins, the tale of Sawney Bean continues to captivate and horrify audiences. It has inspired numerous adaptations in literature, film, and popular culture, often serving as a gruesome cautionary tale about the dark side of human nature. The story's enduring appeal lies in its ability to tap into deep-seated fears about the unknown and the monstrous, as well as its reflection of societal anxieties about crime, punishment, and the breakdown of moral order. The legend of Sawney Bean also serves as a reminder of the power of folklore to shape perceptions and influence culture, illustrating how stories of horror and depravity can become embedded in the collective consciousness.

In examining the tale of Sawney Bean, one can also explore the broader themes of lawlessness and the fragility of civilization. The story of a clan living outside the bounds of society, engaging in acts of extreme violence and cannibalism, highlights the precarious nature of social order and the ever-present possibility of its collapse. It speaks to the fear of the "other" and the ways in which societies construct narratives to define and protect themselves against perceived threats. The Beans' cave, a dark and hidden place filled with the remains of their victims, symbolizes the lurking danger of human savagery and the thin veneer that separates civilization from barbarism.

The legend of Sawney Bean, whether rooted in fact or entirely fictional, continues to be a powerful and disturbing story that resonates with audiences. It challenges us to confront our deepest fears about the capacity for evil within ourselves and others and serves as a grim reminder of the darkness that can lurk beneath the surface of society. As a piece of folklore, it underscores the importance of storytelling in shaping our understanding of the world and our place within it, offering a chilling glimpse into the darker aspects of human nature and the enduring fascination with tales of horror and depravity.

Chapter 30: Vincenzo Peruggia

Vincenzo Peruggia, born on October 8, 1881, in Dumenza, Italy, is most famously known as the man who stole the Mona Lisa from the Louvre Museum in Paris in 1911. This audacious theft, which took place on August 21 of that year, remains one of the most sensational and intriguing art heists in history. Peruggia's actions not only brought him infamy but also catapulted the already-famous painting into an unparalleled realm of global renown, solidifying its status as an icon of Western art. The story of Vincenzo Peruggia is a fascinating tale that intertwines art, nationalism, and the psychology of a man driven by complex motives.

Peruggia's early life in Italy was relatively unremarkable. He trained as a house painter and decorator, a skill that would eventually lead him to Paris in search of better economic opportunities. In Paris, he worked on various projects, including some that involved painting and installing protective glass for artworks in the Louvre. This employment would later provide him with the intimate knowledge of the museum's layout and security systems, which he would exploit in his daring heist.

The theft of the Mona Lisa was meticulously planned and executed with a simplicity that belied its audacity. On the morning of August 21, 1911, Peruggia entered the Louvre, a place he was familiar with due to his previous employment. Disguised in a white smock, similar to those worn by museum staff, he blended in easily with the other workers. Peruggia hid in a small storage closet until the museum was closed to the public. Once he was confident that the museum was empty, he emerged from his hiding place and approached the Salon Carré, where the Mona Lisa was displayed.

The Mona Lisa, painted by Leonardo da Vinci in the early 16th century, was already an iconic masterpiece, revered for its enigmatic expression and unparalleled artistic technique. Its location in the Louvre made it one of the most visited artworks in the world. Peruggia, aware of its value and significance, had selected it as the target of his theft, believing that its removal would not only bring him personal gain but also serve a larger purpose. He carefully lifted the painting from the wall, removed it from its protective case, and carried it to the stairwell. There, he removed the wooden frame and concealed the painting under his smock, exiting the museum unnoticed.

The theft went undetected until the following day when the museum staff discovered the empty space where the Mona Lisa had hung. The news of the stolen painting quickly spread, causing a media frenzy. The French press dubbed the theft "the greatest art theft of the 20th century," and the international attention it garnered only heightened the mystique and allure of the stolen masterpiece. The French police launched an extensive investigation, and the Louvre was closed for a week as detectives combed through the museum for clues. Despite their efforts, the identity of the thief remained a mystery, and the whereabouts of the Mona Lisa unknown.

Peruggia had taken the painting to his modest apartment in Paris, where he kept it hidden in a trunk for over two years. During this time, he lived a relatively quiet life, seemingly unaffected by the massive manhunt and media attention that his crime had generated. His ability to evade capture and maintain the painting's secrecy for such an extended period is a testament to his cunning and resourcefulness. The Mona Lisa's absence from the Louvre created a cultural void, and its return became a matter of international concern.

In December 1913, Peruggia finally attempted to sell the painting. He contacted Alfredo Geri, an art dealer in Florence, under the pretext of wanting to return the painting to its rightful place in Italy. Peruggia's motive, as he later claimed, was rooted in a sense of patriotism. He believed that the Mona Lisa had been stolen by Napoleon and taken to France, and that it was his duty to return the masterpiece to its homeland. This narrative of cultural repatriation, although historically inaccurate, played a significant role in shaping Peruggia's justification for his crime.

Peruggia arranged to meet with Geri and Giovanni Poggi, the director of the Uffizi Gallery, at a hotel in Florence. When he presented the painting, Geri and Poggi quickly realized that it was indeed the original Mona Lisa. They convinced Peruggia to leave the painting with them under the guise of verifying its authenticity. Once Peruggia had departed, they contacted the authorities, leading to his arrest the following day. The Mona Lisa was returned to the Louvre amidst great fanfare and public celebration. The painting's recovery was seen as a triumph of justice, and its theft had only served to increase its fame and mystique.

Peruggia's trial in Italy was a sensational affair, drawing significant media attention. He was portrayed by some as a hero, a patriot who had attempted to reclaim a national treasure for Italy. This narrative of noble intent resonated with the Italian public, and Peruggia was viewed by many as a defender of cultural heritage rather than a common thief. His defense hinged on the argument that he had acted out of patriotic duty, believing that the Mona Lisa rightfully belonged in Italy. Despite these claims, Peruggia was found guilty of theft and sentenced to one year and fifteen days in prison, a relatively lenient sentence considering the magnitude of his crime.

Peruggia's actions and the subsequent trial had a profound impact on the art world and the public's perception of art theft. The Mona Lisa's theft highlighted the vulnerabilities of even the most prestigious institutions and underscored the need for improved security measures to protect cultural treasures. The incident also brought to the forefront the complex issues surrounding cultural ownership and the repatriation of art, topics that continue to be relevant in contemporary discussions about the preservation and restitution of cultural heritage.

Following his release from prison, Vincenzo Peruggia returned to Italy, where he lived a relatively quiet life, working as a painter and decorator. He largely faded into obscurity, his moment of infamy overshadowed by the lasting legacy of the Mona Lisa and its place in art history. Peruggia's motives and the true nature of his intentions remain a subject of debate among historians and scholars. Some view him as a simple opportunist driven by greed, while others believe that he genuinely saw himself as a patriot acting to rectify a historical wrong. Regardless of his motivations, Peruggia's theft of the Mona Lisa stands as one of the most audacious and impactful art crimes in history.

The story of Vincenzo Peruggia and the theft of the Mona Lisa continues to captivate the imagination of the public and has been the subject of numerous books, films, and academic studies. It serves as a fascinating case study in the psychology of crime, the power of art, and the ways in which cultural artifacts can become symbols of national identity and pride. Peruggia's theft, while a criminal act, also underscores the deep emotional and cultural connections that people have with art, and the lengths to which they will go to protect and reclaim their heritage.

The legacy of Vincenzo Peruggia and his audacious heist endures as a testament to the enduring allure of the Mona Lisa and the complex interplay between art, culture, and history. His story reminds us of the profound impact that a single act of theft can have on the world and the ways in which art can transcend time and geography to become an integral part of our collective consciousness. The Mona Lisa's journey from the walls of the Louvre to a modest apartment in Paris and back again has only enhanced its mystique, making it not just a masterpiece of Renaissance art, but a symbol of the enduring power of cultural heritage and the human desire to possess and protect it.

Epilogue

As the final pages of "Legends of Infamy: The Life Stories of Notorious Thieves" come to a close, we find ourselves gazing back into the dim corridors of history, where the shadows of these extraordinary individuals linger. Their stories, woven through the fabric of time, remind us that the line between heroism and villainy is often as thin as a whisper, as delicate as a spider's thread.

We have walked the paths of outlaws and rebels, exploring the lives of those who chose defiance over obedience, who lived by their wits and thrived on the edges of society. Their tales are a testament to the complexities of human nature, revealing a landscape where morality is not always black and white but is painted in shades of gray. Each chapter has peeled back the layers of myth to reveal the flesh and blood behind the legends, offering glimpses into the minds of those who dared to challenge the conventions of their time.

Throughout these pages, we have seen that notoriety is not a simple measure of criminality. It is a reflection of the times, a mirror held up to society's deepest fears and darkest desires. The notorious thieves we have explored were not mere criminals; they were figures who captivated the public imagination, whose lives and deeds continue to echo through the centuries.

Their stories have been told and retold, each time gaining new layers of embellishment and intrigue. From the audacious heists of the Great Train Robbers to the cunning schemes of Charles Ponzi, from the high-seas exploits of Blackbeard to the shadowy escape of D.B. Cooper, these tales remind us of the allure of the forbidden, the romance of rebellion, and the eternal human fascination with those who live outside the law.

But what have we learned from these legends of infamy? Perhaps it is that the nature of crime and punishment is as old as humanity itself, evolving with our societies and cultures. The thieves we've examined were not merely outlaws; they were also products of their environments, shaped by the injustices and opportunities of their times. Their stories force us to question our own values and the systems we uphold, urging us to reflect on the thin line between justice and retribution, order and chaos.

As we close the book on these notorious lives, we are left with a deeper understanding of the human spirit's capacity for ingenuity and audacity. These figures were not content to play by the rules; they sought to rewrite them. In their defiance, we see the complexity of the human condition, the struggle against conformity, and the relentless pursuit of freedom, however fleeting it may be.

Their legacies continue to inspire, to caution, and to entertain. They serve as reminders that the past is never truly past, that the echoes of their deeds continue to shape our present and our future. In studying their lives, we gain insight into the eternal dance between order and chaos, between the law and those who live beyond its reach.

And so, as we turn the final page, we bid farewell to these legends of infamy. Their stories, immortalized in the annals of history, remind us that the pursuit of infamy is as much a part of the human experience as the quest for greatness. In their tales, we find the echoes of our own desires, our own rebellions, and our own dreams of a life lived boldly and without regret.

Farewell to the audacious, the daring, and the defiant. May their stories continue to captivate and inspire, challenging us to see the world from a different perspective, to question the status quo, and to remember that, in the end, it is not the deeds themselves that define us, but the courage to live life on our own terms.

This is the legacy of the notorious thieves, the indelible mark they leave on the tapestry of history. Their stories are ours to remember, to ponder, and to carry forward into the future. For in their infamy, we find the reflections of our own human spirit, ever restless, ever bold, ever reaching for something just beyond the horizon.

The End.